To R

Perley

The True Story Of A New Hampshire Hermit

I hope you enjoy Perley's story!

Shirle Swett

Sketch of Perley Swett Drawn by Arthur Tremblay - 1975
Courtesy of Tony Tremblay

Perley

The True Story Of A New Hampshire Hermit

By Sheila Swett Thompson

Edited by Bob Weekes
Foreword by Ernest Hebert

Published by:
Historical Society of Cheshire County
Keene, New Hampshire
2008

Additional copies available from:
Historical Society of Cheshire County
PO Box 803
Keene, NH 03431
www.hsccnh.org

To contact the author
Sheila Swett Thompson
Sswett@ne.rr.com

Published by:
Historical Society of Cheshire County
Keene, New Hampshire
2008

Copyright © 2008 Sheila Swett Thompson
Cover picture of Perley courtesy of his daughter, Bernice Swett Clark
Interior text design by Tom Davis
ISBN: 978-0-9724478-8-1
Library of Congress Control Number: 2008938263

Perley: The True Story of a New Hampshire Hermit.
All rights reserved. Except for brief excerpts used in reviews, no portion of this work may be reproduced or published without expressed written permission from the author or the author's agent.

First Edition
Printed and bound in the United States of America by Morris Publishing • www.morrispublishing.com • 800-650-7888
1 2 3 4 5 6 7 8 9 10

Foreword
By Ernest Hebert

I first ran into Perley Swett and his legend back in 1968 when I was a student at Keene State College. He'd written a poem called "Housekeeper Wanted," in the style of John Greenleaf Whittier, that was circulating among us English majors. Craig Turner, a friend and fellow student, told me about the time he was deer hunting on Perley's property in Stoddard when he came upon a balsam fir that would make a perfect Christmas tree. Craig started chopping away with his hunting knife when he sensed a presence behind him. He whirled around to find Perley holding paper and pencil. "That's okay, keep cutting," Perley said. "I'm just making out your receipt."

That same year my girlfriend (now wife) and I and another couple visited Perley at his farmhouse. He was very cordial, courtly with the young women. He showed us his gravesite (marked) with a sign that said "Hermit of Taylor Pond." He invited us into his home, which had no electricity and no plumbing. To keep warm in the winter he'd put his feet in the oven of the wood burning stove.

He had a beautiful face, and with his long white hair looked a little bit like a rural version of Albert Einstein. We were charmed by Perley. Years later Perley was the inspiration for Cooty Patterson, a fictional character I developed in several of my books.

But, in fact, my knowledge of Perley was very shallow. It wasn't until I read Sheila Swett's brilliant biography of Perley that I realized he was so much more interesting and complicated than his public persona. Sheila Swett tells a story of ambition, passion, land lust, failure, bitterness, anger, but in the end redemption in old age, and in a prose style that clicks along like a fast-paced novel.

Perley Swett's story is fascinating enough, but Sheila Swett has given us more, glimpses into the lives of scores of the people who touched the old hermit's life, especially Perley's mother and wife, strong women who overcame tremendous odds, including fraud, adultery and incest.

Besides telling us the in-depth story of the old hermit, Sheila Swett uncloaks the mystery behind other local myths, such as the legend of Shinbone Shack in Stoddard.

This book not only adds to our knowledge of Cheshire County (and rural New Hampshire), it's a great read.

Acknowledgments

I am amazed at and thankful for all the help and support I have received over the last six years researching and writing my grandfather's story. I send my deepest appreciation to all those who remember Perley and have lent a picture, recalled a memory, helped with research or shown an interest in this project. Special thanks go to the following:

First and foremost, Bob Weekes who knew Perley and whose encouragement, patience and judicious editing have guided me to produce a story I can be proud of. Without his help there would be no book on the Hermit of Taylor Pond.

Alan Rumrill, Director of the Historical Society of Cheshire County. I'm grateful for his belief that Perley's story should be preserved in the annals of Cheshire County history. Alan's help has been invaluable in creating the best book possible. And my sincere appreciation for the society's willingness to publish my book.

Ernie Hebert for his kind words, encouragement and "ego boost" when I needed it most. His willingness to help a first-time writer meant the world to me.

Quentin White who was always a good and loyal friend to Perley. By preserving all of Perley's personal papers, poetry and diaries for almost thirty years he gave me a wealth of information to work with.

Don and Joyce Healy for sharing information on Florence Brooks Aten and allowing me access to Shinbone Shack and Florence Brooks Aten's lodge.

The Keene Sentinel, Yankee Publishing Inc, The Boston Globe, The Boston Herald, The Schlesinger Library, and The

Manchester Union for allowing me to reprint pictures and quotes.

Tom Davis of Old Mountain Press for his patience, expertise and prompt response in the typesetting of my book.

Anne Faulkner and her husband, Bob King, for welcoming my family and me back to Perley's homestead whenever we descend upon them.

Joan Dempsey who also guided my writing, helping me with the proper way to put my thoughts on paper.

Dr. Shawn Shea, author and noted psychologist, for his insight into Perley's psyche.

Jackie and Bill Cleary for sharing their experience in writing Jackie's book, "Waiting for William," and helping me understand some of Perley's legal battles.

Rick Van Wickler and Lt. Hank Colby for giving me a tour of the Westmoreland House of Corrections.

Raette and Arthur Trombley for providing me a quiet place to work on Perley's story.

My brother, Dan Swett, who always took the time to give me support and sound advice whenever I pestered him for it.

My cousin, David Swett, for sharing his information on family genealogy; and all my aunts, uncles and cousins who took the time to unearth pictures, letters and memories about Perley and his life.

A special posthumous thank you to my father, Maurice Swett, who gave me my interest in family history. Though I never said it to him while he was alive, he was a wonderful father and I wish I could share with him all of the family pictures and history I have uncovered which I know he would have relished.

And, last but with all my love and appreciation, my husband, Dick, and our two wonderful sons, Jake and Sam, who gave me all the time and support I needed to write this book.

Contents

Let me introduce you... 15

Chapter One 43
    Ancestral Ties

Chapter Two 55
    Elsie Jane

Chapter Three 67
    Growing up

Chapter Four 81
    A Marriage of Hope

Chapter Five 91
    Secrets of the Past

Chapter Six 101
    A Visitor

Chapter Seven 113
    Lives Intertwined

Chapter Eight 131
    The End of a Dream

Chapter Nine 143
    It All Comes Crashing Down

Chapter Ten 153
    A Prideful Incarceration

Chapter Eleven 165
    Elsie Jane's Pain

Chapter Twelve 173
    Time to Go

Chapter Thirteen 179
    "I Have Never Found a Companion So
    Companionable as Solitude"

Chapter Fourteen 189
    "Housekeeper Wanted"

Chapter Fifteen 205
    Frugality Rules

Chapter Sixteen 215
    Perley's Poetry

Chapter Seventeen 227
    Paradise Found and Paradise Lost

Chapter Eighteen 235
    A Final Resting Place

Chapter Nineteen 243
    Visitors - Wanted and Unwanted

Chapter Twenty 251
    To Give is to Receive

Chapter Twenty-One 263
    Goodbye Dear Friend

A Final Visit 273

Some postscripts from people who knew Perley 283

Perley's Poetry 287

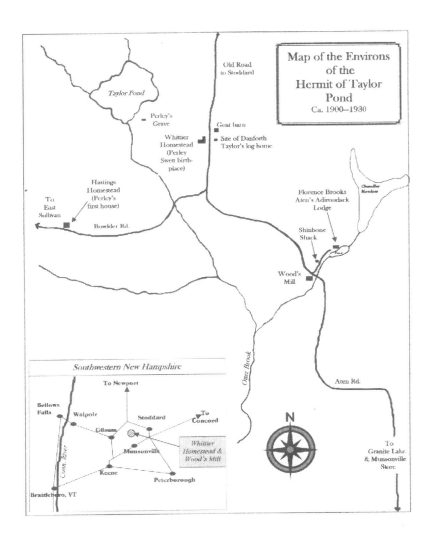

Map of Perley's home and vicinity
Courtesy of Bob Weekes

Perley Edwin Swett (Age 81) - 1971
Courtesy of John Bridges

Let me introduce you...

My grandfather, Perley Swett, dug his own grave, both literally and figuratively. Born during the harsh winter of 1888 in a sparsely populated corner of Stoddard, New Hampshire, he began a journey from cradle to grave that would never take him far from his roots. Growing up in a family that scratched its meager existence from rock-bound farmland, Perley learned the meaning of "make-do" at an early age. With little schooling (he was needed on the farm) and even less exposure to society at large, Perley grew up with a deeply ingrained puritanical view of right and wrong, a view which never wavered or left room for imperfections in those around him. His self-righteous adherence to these values set him on a course that would leave him isolated and alone. His would be a long, lonely and sometimes tragic journey that in the end produced little to comfort him except a herd of goats and the land he held so dear.

Grampa wanted to make sure that he would never be forced to leave the New Hampshire farm he was born on...and which had become his refuge...even in death. Worried that his family might ignore his written instructions and bury him in a more conventional spot, (He was concerned, as he put it, that *"lawyers would prefer to please the living rather than honor a dead man's wishes."*) Perley felt he had to take matters into his own hands. And, at age seventy-five, he did just that - with a pick and shovel.

Though ten more years would pass before Perley would occupy this hand-dug grave, his curious act would cement his reputation as "The Hermit of Taylor Pond." Up until that point the word "hermit" might have come up now and then as the town's residents discussed his peculiarities, but mostly Grampa was just thought of as an eccentric recluse. Small towns can be quite accepting of their quirky characters; with a certain pride of ownership, they become inured to any oddities exhibited by a life-long resident.

Down at Jack Hammond's little general store (the only store in the town of Sullivan, New Hampshire) someone might have been heard to comment, "Yep, Ol' Perley Swett is so cheap, he charged his own brother twenty-five cents to park in his field to go fishin." This was usually muttered with a lop-sided grin, as if to imply that "he's an odd duck, but he is *our* odd duck!"

At birth, my grandfather had been given the melodious name of Perley Edwin Swett. In the last few years of his life, he also became known by several different monikers: The Hermit of Stoddard, The Hermit of Hidden Hollow and The Hermit of Devil's Paradise. *"How easy to become a famous hermit,"* he once said, *"just by not moving or dying."*

The narrow dirt road that led to his isolated home deep in the forest went unplowed during the brutal New Hampshire winters and was thick with sticky mud or totally washed out much of the rest of the year. There were very few days when my family would be able to make the difficult trip to Grampa's home. For that reason, I can still remember the excitement I felt when my father woke me early one summer morning in 1962, saying, *"The weather looks good today; we ought to be able to make it up to Grampa's."*

To prepare for our trip, we loaded up the truck with needed supplies along with a gingerbread cake and blueberry pie that my mother baked as a special treat for Grampa. As he aged, Grampa had to rely on friends and relatives to bring him his groceries since he could no longer walk the three miles through the woods to the nearest store. He never did own or learn to drive a motorized vehicle.

As my father and I waved goodbye to my mother to begin our journey, I climbed up onto the torn seat of Dad's 1957 Willys pickup truck. I was only seven years old at the time and yet I still recall the pungent scent of gas, motor oil and sawdust all mingled into something I actually found quite pleasant. I moved aside my father's gasoline soaked gloves, which were missing the ends of a couple of fingers, and stuffed the loose wool batting around the metal springs of the torn seat so I wouldn't get jabbed by the sharp points as we bounced along. Metal chains lay curled up like snakes on the floor of the truck. There was a 'come along' and jack behind the seat. These would come in handy in case we got stuck in a ditch. A chainsaw always accompanied us too, since it was likely fallen trees or large branches would block sections of this old trail. Never one to waste anything, Dad would hop out, cut up what was now firewood and toss it in the back of the truck.

My father devoted a good part of his life to sawing, splitting and stacking wood to burn, either for Grampa or for us at home. Cordwood had always been the first line of defense against the long New Hampshire winters. Dad entered his eightieth year before he finally replaced his old wood furnace with one fueled by propane. When we asked him why he had waited so long to do this he said, *"Until I reached eighty it was no problem to get enough wood to burn but I'm not as young as I used to be and thought it best to prepare for the future."*

I can still remember my nervousness when my father would fire up the big three foot circular saw blade driven by a fan belt system hooked to the back of his 1952 Ford

Tractor. No safety guards in those days, just that mean saw blade whining and spinning as he sliced through the logs, reducing them to stove length pieces.

As we continued on to Grampa's, my father veered the truck off the main road onto the aptly named "Bowlder Road." Our route took us by my great uncle Martin's house and past the entrance to Bolster Pond where we sometimes went fishing. Next, we came to the red, one-room Schoolhouse #3 where my father spent his first eight years of school, then up past the house of former New Hampshire Attorney General, Gardner C. Turner.

At this point the grass began to grow down the middle of the dirt road and civilization was left behind. It was like traveling over a washboard which threatened to shake loose every nut and bolt under the chassis. Likely it was roads like this that made someone realize that belts to harness children in their seats would be a good idea. Without one, I ricocheted all over that truck!

We were quickly swallowed up by the dense forest as the thoroughfare became a mere tunnel through the trees. I felt we were heading into an ominous jungle with whatever my child's imagination could think of hiding behind every tree and rock. The trip was exciting but I also worried that my father and I would end up stranded in the middle of miles and miles of nowhere.

The road had turned into little more than two parallel ruts running between ancient stonewalls which had stood quiet sentinel for the last two hundred years. Driving a straight line was impossible. We lurched and bounced along as my father expertly maneuvered around rocks that were exposed where gravel had long ago washed away.

On the way to Grampa's house I asked my father to stop at the weathered remains of another family farm. In the way that small towns have of naming their homesteads, it was known as the "Old Hastings Place" even though the Hastings hadn't lived there for almost one hundred years. This abandoned house, two miles closer to "civilization" than the one we were heading toward, was also owned and occupied by my grandfather Perley when he was first raising his family. It was the place where my own father was born and grew up. Now this dilapidated house was in such a state of disrepair that my father and I could only stand outside and imagine what it had once looked like. The chimney had caved in taking part of the roof with it. Peeking through the window, we saw an old, forgotten piano that mice had chewed on leaning toward the basement as the floor bowed under it.

Before leaving, we stopped to pick wild blueberries from the many bushes that had grown up around the house. We then climbed back into the truck and continued on our way, hoping we wouldn't meet another vehicle on the narrow road. If another vehicle did come along, it would take no small amount of maneuvering to pass, but we'd somehow get by each other with a "how doin'" and a wave "hello."

Finally, we passed over a small brook (thankfully the rickety wooden bridge crossing it was still intact) and up the last incline to Grampa's house.

One newspaper journalist (Charles E. Claffey, The Boston Globe 1962) who courageously had made this same trip described the route this way: *"The rustic road rises steeply near the end of the jolting journey, and a natural arch formed by towering maple trees opens into a sprawling, hilltop meadow."* Many of Grampa's visitors were forced to leave their vehicles at the bottom of this steep, washed out hill and walk the rest of the way up to his house.

As the house and old barn came into view, we were greeted by Grampa's goats who stopped their munching long enough to inspect the company that had just arrived. They knew they were in for a treat of crackers and always swarmed around any visiting vehicle. We pulled up in front of the house and before we even got out of the truck, there was Grampa Perley standing in the slanted doorway.

In my excitement to see him, I swung the truck door wide and jumped down from the seat. Landing unexpectedly in a pile of goat droppings, I found myself staring directly into the face of an enormous, dirty white "monster" with gnashing teeth and the tongue of an anteater. Being small for my age, I stood no more than eye to eye with that goat. Having him stare me in the face, nudging me for a treat with his wet mouth and sharp horns, was not one of my fondest memories of visiting my grandfather.

The herd seemed bigger than ever and, in fact, numbered over one hundred. It was an amazing sight to see Grampa surrounded by so many goats clamoring for attention and treats. (After I read the book, "Heidi," I would never again look at Grampa silhouetted against his old barn without thinking of him as "The Grandfather" in the book. I always felt Heidi and I shared a common bond. I wonder how she *really* felt about those goats?)

Despite my personal opinion, Grampa loved his goats. They were never penned in when outside but were allowed to roam freely. Usually they all found their way back to the barn for refuge by nightfall. If one was late returning home, Grampa worried and waited for it as would a father whose daughter was out on her first date. He would gather his flashlight and a box of crackers and go in search of the wayward pet. Sometimes he covered five to six miles before giving up for the night. Invariably the next morning the missing goat would be back, bleating for some attention and the inevitable scolding for making his owner worry. And if any of his goats were sick or injured, Grampa sat up nights in the old barn, nursing them. At times he even brought a particularly ailing pet into his house to stay warm in front of the woodstove.

Grampa could tell you their names and heritage as someone would his prized thoroughbreds. *"This here one is Daisy,"* he would rasp. *"She's the daughter of Betty who was one of the twins from Minnie. Minnie was the one who came home on her knees one day after being caught in a trap."* The goats kept him company and followed him around like loyal and loving pets. Their self-esteem was also of concern to Grampa. As he wrote to one young pen-pal, *"I won't tell them you called them 'sheep' as doubtless they would consider it an insult."*

It became a tradition for Grampa to give all his visitors a package of Saltine crackers so both young and old could feed the goats. Unfortunately, my visit was not to be an exception. He gave me a package of crackers and then called out in his rattling voice: *"Hayaaa, hayaaa, come on, come on, hayaaa,"* and all the goats came running. I've always thought that it was a pretty good test of my courage that I didn't run screaming to my father when I saw that herd of goats bearing down on me. I stood my ground, waiting for the onslaught. I would never have admitted to anyone that feeding those goats was the last thing I felt like doing! Pride and wanting Grampa's favor forced me to suppress my fears. So I fed those greedy animals their crackers, hoping I would still have all my fingers when I was done.

But I still loved visiting Grampa Perley, not just for the excitement that these adventures held for a young girl but also because these were special times spent with my father. When my brothers did come along on these visits, it was usually because there was work to be done. They helped my father hay the fields. I've seen pictures of the loose hay piled high on the old truck and I admired not only how they were able to get it all up there but also keep it up there. My brother Dan had that job, balancing on top of the pile to anchor the load. I've often wondered, though, what kept *him* from falling off. When their hot and itchy job was done, Perley would dip into an old Koolaid package where he kept his change and give each of my brothers a quarter for their day of hard work.

Dan remembered those haying days only too well, *"Usually going to Perley's meant a long day of hard, dirty work. I remember unloading truckloads of hay in the old barn. Grampa would walk out to see how we were doing, bent over somewhat, leaning on a cane. I remember watching from the hayloft as I helped unload the hay that I had two hours earlier meticulously piled on our old flatbed truck. Grampa would be standing in the doorway to the barn, in a ray of sunshine, and in that sunshine I could see surrounding him all the dust and chaff from the hay we were unloading. Now I was still quite young, perhaps ten or twelve, but understood work and pay well enough even then to know that the 25 cents that Grampa would ultimately give us would be far less than the amount of work we did was worth."* All that effort is but a memory now, as those hay fields have long since grown back to woodland.

My father, Maurice Swett, was Perley's third son and, like Perley himself, was a "Jack of all trades." He single-handedly cleared his land, built his house and made repairs on anything that broke, just like his father and ancestors had. I never remember a repairman coming to our house. If my Dad couldn't fix something, it was probably beyond repair. For Perley had taught all his sons to be self-sufficient men used to hard work and capable of working expertly with their hands. In fact, each of Perley's six children grew up to be fine, upstanding citizens with families to be proud of. As a child, I was blissfully unaware of the unresolved tension between Grampa Perley and his adult children. It wasn't until much later in my life, as I puzzled over the reasons why

Perley

Grampa chose to live the way he did, that I came to learn that Perley's relationship with his children was quite troubled.

"Old Hastings Place" - Sullivan, NH
Swett family home deserted and falling in around 1962
Courtesy of Bernice Swett Clark

"Bowlder Road"
Leading to Perley's ancestral home in Stoddard, NH
Courtesy of Jean Batchelder

Perley standing in the doorway of the shed leading into his house
Courtesy of Quentin White

Whittier/Swett homestead, Stoddard, NH
Taken 1928 - Courtesy of Historical Society of Cheshire County

Perley, Sheila (the author), her father Maurice Swett, and the goats

Perley

    I suppose if one had never laid eyes on a hermit, Grampa looked the part to perfection. At the age of seventy-four he was slightly stooped, his weakened frame bending over his ever-present walking stick. Depending on the season, Grampa's hair and beard were either short and ragged, usually trimmed by his own hand, or left to grow long for the slight protection they gave against the frigid New Hampshire winters. Though sparse on top, flowing tufts of white hair grew full around the sides of his head. Blending in with his beard and moustache, they gave him a resemblance to Albert Einstein.

    The top of Grampa's head was bald and mottled brown from years of working in the sun. Hard work and the aging process had deepened the wrinkles which gave his face so much character. His twinkling blue eyes, slightly milky from the beginnings of cataracts, constantly watered, hinting at the sadness that was never too far below the surface. Yet this contrasted curiously with the impression of merriment created by the permanent creases at the corners of his eyes which suggested that his droll humor could match wits with any man. In fact, Grampa was often amused by others startled reactions upon first meeting him. Finally, the loss of most of Grampa's teeth earlier in life gave his cheeks a sunken look when he was clean shaven. Taken together, all this made him a most proper hermit.

    Grampa always dressed in layers of time-worn and patched clothing. In the heat of the summer a dirty white t-shirt sufficed, with stained tan pants which always sagged around his waist and were only held up by suspenders. They would be repaired many times before being ready for the rag pile. As cold weather replaced the heat of summer, he added long underwear and a flannel shirt, buttoned up to the neck, with either a sweater or coat patched at or completely missing the elbows.

To top off his ensemble, Grampa wore a colorful red kerchief tied neatly around his neck. His one concession to modern clothing were black, high-top Keds canvas sneakers. Most days Grampa walked several miles, so his shoes were the only items that he felt were necessary to replace regularly.

If a new article of clothing was needed, Grampa would spend hours poring over a Sears/Roebuck or Montgomery Ward catalog searching for the best value. He seldom could get to a store to shop so any purchase of winter wear had to be planned well in advance as it might be several weeks, once the snow came, before Grampa could get his mail. Appearance didn't matter as long as the clothing was sturdy and suited the purpose of the work and the season at hand.

Sometimes a sympathetic visitor, hoping to upgrade his torn and tattered apparel, brought Grampa a new shirt or sweater. He promptly stored them away as being "too fancy" to wear. Mostly his wardrobe consisted of whatever old clothes he found that had been packed away in the house for years. When he got a touch of rheumatism in one shoulder, Grampa remedied the problem by cutting a sleeve off another old coat and pinning it over the sleeve of the coat he was wearing, thereby keeping his sore shoulder extra warm.

Grampa's niece, Elva Swett Frazier, told me how she once asked him why in the world he dressed in rags when he could certainly afford better. *"If I don't dress like this,"* Grampa told her with a sly grin, *"I won't look like a 'real' hermit and that is what people come to see."*

Every few months Grampa soaked the layers of dirt from his clothes in the bathtub outside and then draped the wet items over whatever was handy to dry them in the sun. Entries in Grampa's diaries always made note of when he changed into his "winter underwear" or when he took a bath and put on clean clothes. Obviously, he felt it was a noteworthy event and was by no means a daily occurrence. *"My bathtub is outdoors under the eaves,"* he wrote one January to a friend, *"and I certainly do hate to use it, especially in below freezing weather!"* Despite his ragged garb, I don't recall ever thinking that my grandfather was unclean in body though that is obviously the impression he was trying to create when he jokingly added, *"Creosote has been leaking onto the floor from the stove pipe. When I get around to wash my feet, maybe about June, I may need to use kerosene!"* Whether his mode of dress was planned or just practical, Perley enjoyed poking fun at himself and his attire.

After my dreaded encounter with the goats, and still sporting all ten of my fingers, we headed toward Grampa's house for a visit.

The house had been built in 1801 and now, along with the owner, was definitely showing its age. Several of the small sheds and outbuildings had already collapsed into piles of rubble. Even as a child I knew that Grampa's house had gone beyond the point of being just 'run down'. It had a mysterious, other-worldly feel...as if time had stopped a century earlier at this remote hilltop farm. There were no traces of paint or any visible signs that repairs had been made to Grampa's home for almost a century. Weathered grey, the wood shingles covering the house were curled and brittle and chewed by the goats as high as they could reach. So much needed fixing I doubt if Grampa would have known where to begin. He explained his predicament: *"Plenty to be done, but the inclination seems gone. Partly old age, a large part laziness, and some from seeing a lot of work done when I were 'ambitious' were only labor wasted. Several acres I had fairly well cleared of stone is now brush or woodland."*

No manicured lawn surrounded the house. The goats had the job of cutting the grass, giving the yard the uneven look of a bad haircut. Tufts of flowers planted by a loving hand many years earlier now blossomed only sporadically among the weeds.

At one time, Perley's family had an extensive working orchard from which fruit was harvested to preserve or sell. Now only a few surviving apple trees grew randomly in overgrown fields. Any apples they produced were too small and mealy for anyone other than the goats and deer to eat. Rusting farm equipment, abandoned under the trees many years before, were now frozen for eternity as a testament to the last task for which they were used...and then left.

In true New England fashion, stonewalls outlined the fields, placed there two hundred years ago as the earliest settlers cleared the land to plant crops for their families. Perley and his ancestors had spent many back-breaking years trying to clear the land of rocks, seemingly to no avail. Somehow more always worked their way to the surface. Huge boulders, too big to move, jutted out of the ground near the old barn. The baby goats used them to play "king of the hill."

To the left of the doorway to Grampa's house was a dilapidated overhang of roof that gave sparse protection to the assortment of dooryard paraphernalia piled under it. Firewood took up one side and the other was occupied by an antiquated wood treadmill. Originally it was meant to operate a piece of farm machinery, powered by farm animals. But now it was used only to exercise grandchildren and other young visitors. Old sap buckets, a rusting bed frame, a scythe hanging from a rusty nail, and other discarded items finished off the pile. At the front was the antique claw-foot bathtub that doubled as a watering trough for the goats.

We entered the house through what was left of a chain of connected sheds which had been added on many years before to store the family's supply of firewood. Half of them had fallen in around the 1950s, the other half looked ready to go at any moment. My father had to duck down to fit his six-foot-frame through the decaying doorway. No longer able to close because the shed had settled and shifted over the years, the door offered no protection from the elements and did nothing more than add a tired support to the corner of the entrance.

We carefully wove our way through the darkened entry between stacks of firewood which lined both sides of the narrow passage. There was no flooring in this section, only large irregular granite boulders serving as a walkway. We were forced to step carefully. This was tricky business until our eyes adjusted from the bright sunlight outside to the darkness of the windowless shed. The ceiling was low and adults had to choose between looking up to avoid bumping their heads or down to avoid stumbling on the uneven floor.

A boxed-in, hand-dug well stood in the corner on our right. This was where Grampa, and his ancestors before him, got all the water needed for their daily chores. In a letter to a friend, Grampa wrote that only once or twice in the one hundred years his family lived there did it ever go dry. He'd built a wooden cover for the well only after a fox had fallen into it and he had to fish it out with a bucket. Years earlier, Grampa had set up a pulley system over the well to make it easier to raise the heavy buckets of water. Sometimes the water in the well froze during the coldest parts of the winter. When this happened he had to weight the bucket with rocks and drop it in the well to break through the ice. There was never any plumbing in the house, which, of course, meant no bathroom. Instead, as a reporter for Yankee Magazine once described it, there was an old half-mooner out back that had a tilt the leaning Tower of Pisa would have been proud of. The door of the privy was not attached but was simply propped against one corner. Clearly privacy was not something a hermit worried about.

From the shed we stepped up into the main house and I felt as though I passed back in time. Though the first room we entered had once been the kitchen, there was no refrigerator, stove, dishwasher or other modern appliance one might expect to see. Because electric lines stopped more than two miles before reaching Grampa's house, there were no lights to switch on either. This did not seem to bother Grampa. As he explained, *"I seem to survive fairly well without electricity and some other things that would be appreciated but not necessary to survival."*

One of the first things I became aware of was the smell...a musty, stale odor from layers of dust and soot which were never stirred by fresh air. It was not necessarily unpleasant, just...ancient. I encountered it again as an adult when I visited an elderly woman whose house had also been closed up and cluttered for many years. I would not have thought it possible to remember a scent from thirty years before, but suddenly I was transported back in my memories to Grampa's house and realized what I didn't know then. This was the smell a house took on when it was left to grow old and uncared for, like its owner.

What greeted us now was a room stuffed wall to wall with the remnants of past occupants. For his convenience, Grampa lived in just one of the four rooms on the bottom floor of his house; the remaining rooms and two loft rooms upstairs were used for "storage." The hand dug, dirt basement was off limits, the story being that it was full of snakes and other creepy, crawly things.

Perley's one-room living quarters served not only as his kitchen, but his bedroom, dining room and "office" as well. The house was not insulated and the only source of heat during the long, freezing winters was one small woodstove which required refilling every two hours during the coldest nights. It would entail too much work to try to heat the entire house for just himself so, for comfort, Grampa positioned his cot, a "hired man's bed," directly next to the woodstove. Firewood was stacked in every nook and cranny to be close at hand so the nightly dash to fill the stove could be accomplished as quickly as possible. In a letter to an acquaintance he wrote that on *"some of the coldest nights the goats all may shiver some in the barn. Maybe less than I do in the house. Temperature only reaches 40-50 above in the kitchen on cold days."*

Many a winter eve Perley sat in his chair in front of the stove, begging its warmth to envelop him while a threadbare blanket hugged his shoulders. He would prop his feet as close to the heat as good sense allowed. Asked by one visitor if he kept warm during the cold months he replied, *"I wouldn't say I keep warm - keep from freezing though."*

Even though the day was balmy when my father and I made our visit, the stove was lit since it was the only way Grampa could cook his meals. A pot of something, probably potatoes or soup, was simmering on top. When a gust of wind blew down the chimney, smoke from the woodstove escaped in a puff and made my eyes water.

During the day Grampa relied on what little sunlight could squeeze its way through two small, grime-streaked windows. At night kerosene lamps marginally brightened the rooms. I don't remember any color in his house...everything seemed to be in shades of brown and gray. But, as Grampa reasoned, *"God made daylight and darkness, one for working and one for sleeping,"* and that was the schedule he followed.

Under the layers of dirt the walls were decorated with a design of climbing roses on ancient wallpaper. A soot-streaked, once white painted mantel hung above the fireplace that the stove was now set into. When the house had a woman's touch, I imagined that family pictures and a canning jar filled with violets would have been sitting on top. An embroidered pillow with a proverb extolling some puritan work ethic lay abandoned on top of an old bureau, probably the handiwork of Perley's mother or sisters.

A narrow pathway ran through the center of the room. We picked our way between boxes, worn furniture and old junk or treasures, depending on one's viewpoint. Over the years Grampa had sold many items out of his house to anyone who happened by and saw something to his liking. The visitor was thrilled to buy an antique for very little cost and Grampa was happy thinking he had passed off a piece of junk to some unsuspecting city slicker.

There was hardly an open spot on the floor or furniture that was not covered with something, usually several 'somethings' stacked one on top of the other. One of Perley's poems, written more than ten years before my visit, was titled "Housekeeper Wanted." From the looks of his home it was clear to me that no one ever accepted the position. And Grampa had also accepted the status quo by this point, saying simply, *"Don't know when I'll ever get this housework done."*

Clutter accumulates quickly when a family of pack-rats has lived continuously in the same house for over one hundred years. Letters, diaries, pictures, newspapers and magazines all ended up on Perley's large kitchen table which, at an earlier time, accommodated the entire Swett clan for Thanksgiving Dinner. By the time of my visit it was piled high in disarray. Yet Grampa had his own filing system and always knew exactly where everything was even though he never put his papers in order or threw anything away. He just kept piling more on top, much like a compost pile. Brought up to let nothing go to waste, Grampa even saved the interior wax paper wrapping from each box of Saltines the goats devoured. He used these to line his dinner plate, sparing himself the job of having to wash dishes.

Perley

Old Campbell's soup cans were especially evident. Canned soup, easily stored and prepared, was Perley's main source of nutrition. He also used the reverse side of their labels as writing paper, jotting down correspondence on them. Many a friend or relative left Grampa's house with a poem written on the back of a Campbell's soup label. His favorite variety was vegetable beef which he sometimes ate for breakfast, lunch and dinner. Being thoroughly familiar with its ingredients and consistency, when he felt the company was getting a little <u>less</u> stingy with its beef, Grampa wrote Campbell a rather lengthy testimonial in verse. He seemed to be questioning whether this unusual abundance of meat in their soup was directly due to the loss of any workhorses recently. (See "A Testimonial to the Campbell Soup Company" in Perley's Poetry)

Being of small stature, Grampa looked almost childlike as he settled into his spot behind that cluttered table, his bald head barely visible to me above the mounds of paper. My father sat in the chair by the stove. That left me with only one place to sit, the edge of Grampa's rope bed in the corner. The only support the mattress had were ropes strung across the low wooden frame. This caused the worn, feather-filled mattress to sag so low in the middle it was all I could do to keep from toppling over into its molded center. The pillow also had a permanent indentation from Grampa's head. If the sheets were ever white at one time, they were now a brownish gray. I doubt they were ever taken off the bed and washed. A single, olive green, scratchy wool blanket sat on top, and seemed hardly adequate to keep out the nightly chill.

My father and grandfather immediately launched into a discussion about Grampa's latest land transaction, the quality of the hay that was recently cut or the number of cords of wood accumulated so far for the winter ahead. Feeling momentarily ignored, my eyes wandered around the room and I became lost in thought. It was tempting to touch and investigate everything, but I sat there quietly as I was expected to do. Instead I let my eyes do the exploring while my imagination soared.

At seven, the enticing possibilities of hidden treasures seemed endless to me. Hanging on the wall was an old telephone that didn't look anything like our phone at home. I learned later it was only a decoration, a non-working relic from the past. A more modern phone was buried somewhere under the piles of papers. In front of the old phone a spool of fly paper hung from the ceiling. It had long ago lost its stickiness but still had hundreds of dried flies firmly attached. At the time it did not occur to me to pass judgment on this general lack of cleanliness. I simply accepted it as the way things were at Grampa's house and Grampa accepted it as the way things had always been.

A Montgomery Ward catalog dating from the 1930s sat on a shelf as if it had just been used a week earlier. Boxes stacked almost to the ceiling were even more exciting and mysterious because they were filled with the unknown. Yellowed newspapers had been piled so close to the stove I was amazed that Grampa's house never burned down.

I noticed there were many old calendars hanging on the walls, each stacked on the same nail, one in front of another. They included day-to-day reminders of past events jotted down years ago as the occupants of the house went about their daily lives. Perhaps Grampa could not bear to part with these chronicles of a once busy household. The top calendar was already several years out of date and I did not see any that were current. Did Grampa give up keeping track of the years going by?

A magazine cover of a well-endowed, scantily clad bathing beauty had been hung next to the calendars. If I recall correctly, Grampa introduced this pin-up girl to some of his visitors as his girlfriend. Even as a child I knew this was meant as a joke, but it made me wonder about Grampa's wife. I never knew my grandmother, who died many years before I was born. Grampa never spoke of her and neither did my father. I got the impression that perhaps she was not a subject for discussion...

Grampa lived another ten years after this particular visit and in those years we made many more sojourns to call on him. And while vivid memories of him persisted into my adulthood, the unanswered questions about his unusual lifestyle grew. Who was this man? How did he become estranged from family and friends, isolated from society to the point that he chose to live out his life alone, deep in the wilderness in the company only of his pet goats? What twists and turns did his life take that led him to become "The Hermit of Taylor Pond?" After spending the last few years searching for the answers to those and many more questions, I decided that what I had gathered was worth sharing. This, the true story of a New Hampshire hermit, is my grandfather's story.

Perley and his goats
standing in the entryway to his home
Courtesy of Charlie Wilder

Perley looking dapper after a haircut and shave
Next to one of his old treadmills
Courtesy of Jean Batchelder

Perley at his kitchen table
Courtesy of Quentin White

Perley in his "common room"
Courtesy of the Manchester Union newspaper
Dated December 27, 1961

The old outhouse
Courtesy of Bob Weekes

Perley Swett

Chapter One
Ancestral Ties

Perley Edwin Swett lived the majority of his eighty-five years within a two mile radius, seldom ever traveling very far from the place he was born. His ancestral home in Stoddard, New Hampshire, was tucked back several miles into the woods and situated at the secluded, outer-most point where the boundaries of three small towns happened to intersect. Perley chose to remain in that remote section of town even as he reluctantly watched all his neighbors move away.

The town of Stoddard was incorporated in 1774, just prior to the start of the American Revolution. It was officially named after Colonel Sampson Stoddard but had previously been known as the town of 'Limerick' and also 'Monadnock Number Seven' due to its close proximity to Mount Monadnock.

Alan F. Rumrill, Director of the Historical Society of Cheshire County and lifelong resident of Stoddard, described the town's earlier years: "Stoddard was an agricultural town from the beginning. The first white settlers arrived in the 1760s to farm the rocky soil. The farms were successful and the farmers prospered for almost a century. The town reached its peak of agricultural production in the 1820s as the farm families sold wool and produce to the local storekeepers and in the urban centers of New Hampshire and Massachusetts. The thin soil soon became depleted, however, and the hill farms of southwest New Hampshire could not compete with the produce being shipped east from New York and farms to the west after the construction of the Erie Canal and then the railroads. The slow trickle of emigration became a flood of farm families leaving town after the end of the Civil War."

"Stoddard was also home to 19th century industries, but those could not survive either. A thriving glass industry provided bottles for markets throughout the northeast for thirty years during the mid 1800s and numerous woodenware factories populated the riverbanks throughout the town. Poor roads and expensive transportation costs (the railroad was never constructed to Stoddard) spelled doom for these livelihoods as well."

Stoddard is less populated today than it was one hundred years ago. The town had reached its peak in 1820 with 1,203 residents. During the early 1900s, when Perley was a young boy, the town had already lost more than two-thirds of it's residents. The population had dropped to 367. After World War II the country continued to experience a steady erosion of rural farms. Agricultural living was more difficult and often less productive financially than factory jobs in the cities. Perley wrote to a friend in 1952 that there *"used to be farms and buildings scattered all over this end of town, where there are now no others nearby."* The town's population was at a low of just 146 in 1960.

Around the year 1792 Danforth Taylor rode into town on horseback and became the first settler on the land that was to be occupied by only two families for almost two hundred years...land that eventually would become Perley's home. With the help of his neighbors, Danforth built a split-ash log cabin across the road from the spot where Perley's house still stands. Danforth and his family spent the next eight years clearing the land and setting stone walls. Neighbors assisted them in raising a great barn for their stock, a barn which remained standing for almost two hundred years until it was torn down in the late 1970s. This was the same barn which had housed Perley's goats.

The Taylors had twelve children, all but the first two born at their home in Stoddard. "Squire" Taylor, as he came to be known, found the cabin too small for his growing family and decided to build a larger home on the adjoining lot across the road. A pond on the property still bears his name.

As was typical for the time, Danforth built a center chimney cape with four rooms on the bottom floor and two loft rooms running the length of the upstairs. The central chimney accommodated three fireplaces. It was a comfortable home and well built for that time.

In 1837 Danforth sold the family farm to a son, Jonas Taylor. After a long life, Danforth Taylor died in 1858. His wife of sixty-eight years, Tabitha, died the following year at the age of eighty-nine. They are buried in the old Stoddard Cemetery on Dow Hill.

The Stoddard Town History described all the Taylor children as upstanding members of the community. They became sawmill owners, successful farmers and even politicians. But it was George Taylor, grandson to Danforth, who made the family name known not only in America, but in other parts of the world as well.

At the age of nineteen young George went west to seek his fortune and settled in Rochester, New York. Here he met a young man whose father was an early thermometer manufacturer and, in 1851, the two pooled their resources, skills and energy to start their own manufacture of thermometers.

In a few months the firm moved to larger quarters and business increased rapidly. George's younger brother, Frank, joined him and the Taylor Brothers firm was born. Eventually, it became the Taylor Instrument Company and was one of the most important industries in Rochester. It is still in business today, now a part of MicroMod Automation, an international corporation which produces a wide range of Taylor products for home and industry.

On October 4, 1864, during Abraham Lincoln's presidency, Jonas sold his ancestral home in Stoddard to Jonathan Harvey Whittier, Perley's grandfather. Jonathan, as was quoted in his obituary, was considered *"an industrious and worthy citizen of strictly temperance habits."*

The Whittiers were another early New England family, many of whom had settled principally around Haverhill, Massachusetts. Many of the original Whittiers were Quakers, the most famous being John Greenleaf Whittier, Perley's cousin several times removed. Perley would often allude to his relationship to "the Quaker Poet," though their first common ancestor dates back to Joseph Whittier in 1669. Certainly not a close connection but hoping to be known as a writer of verse himself someday, Perley wanted to be sure it was acknowledged that he was related to this famous poet. He even went so far as to use the pen name, Pearl Whittier, when he signed letters and poetry. Perley was always proud of the fact and boasted that his *"ancestors seem to be all New England Yankees. Though can't quite claim they came over in Mayflower, think it was already overloaded."*

Jonathan and his wife, Mary Andrews, moved into the old Taylor homestead with their three young daughters, Almina Mahala, Lydia May and Elsie Jane, who was destined to become Perley's mother. The Whittiers were thrilled to own their first home. Like many young couples, Jonathan and Mary were eager to be settled and provide a good life for themselves and their children and become part of the small community.

The Whittiers soon discovered they had a most curious neighbor at that time, Rosina Delight Richardson Wood. Rosina was the third child born to Mary (Huntley) and

Nathaniel Richardson of Marlow, New Hampshire. The Marlow Town History described all three children as being *"inclined to corpulence to a remarkable degree."* Rosina was the only one to reach maturity. Though she was a normal weight of six pounds at birth, by the time she was ten months old she was tipping the scales at fifty pounds. By age seven she weighed about two hundred pounds. Rosina was hired as the "Fat Lady" for the famous P.T.Barnum Museum in New York around 1862. Conflicting reports gave her weight as ranging between 515 and 765 pounds with her height being just five feet, three inches.

After Rosina left circus life behind, she married John A. Wood in 1869, which is likely how she became acquainted with the Whittier family. J.A.Wood was listed as a part owner of a sawmill, located less than a mile south of Jonathan and Mary's home. Rosina apparently became a good friend of the family as her gold-framed picture graced the wall of Perley's ancestral home for almost one hundred years. Perley liked to tell anyone who asked about the picture that his mother said that Rosina had to enter the house sideways to fit through the front door. Rosina passed away in 1878 at the age of forty-five.

Because Jonathan Whittier had no sons, his girls were expected to do more than just "woman's work." Not only did they need to help their mother with household chores but they also had to work in the fields alongside their father. Elsie Jane, the middle daughter, was especially well-suited for this type of labor and enjoyed the time spent with her father.

In a diary Elsie Jane kept in 1875 when she was fifteen, she describes in truncated style some of her days working and living on the farm:

"Today I go with my steers and help break road and draw up load of wood

Today I commenced my gingham dress
Father drawing bark to the tamry
Today is so cold that Mother haint a going to wash
Today Mother washed and I hung out clothes and froze my fingers
I iron today and help father handle wood
Today I saw and chop and split wood
Today Mr. Colony sent for me to work in his mill
Father and I go down to boil sap but he is sick with the measles
Today I am sick and can scarcely work
Today I go to town and carry 17 quarts of blueberries (to sell)
We furrow our potato piece and plant our first potatoes, I draw manure
Today I worked all day in the potato field. Mell hired me to pick his potato bugs, pays me .10c
Mother and me dig potatoes, we dig 8 1/4 barrels full; it is hot, we dig 20½ bushels
Today I go out and hoe corn, I set a hen, I bake some mince pies"

From her diary entries it appears Elsie Jane could shoulder a heavy work load.

The Stoddard Town History mentions that as Jonathan Whittier neared sixty, he *"could wield a scythe and bend his prayer-handles like a man of thirty."* Shortly thereafter, the family was dealt a devastating blow when, at the age of fifty-eight, Jonathan went out for supplies and never returned.

Perley would often recount the story of how his grandfather Whittier was lost one bleak wintry night in 1876, just after Christmas. Perhaps it illustrated to Perley how easily a life could be lost when living alone in the harsh wilderness.

On that fateful day, a storm was threatening but the family was low on supplies. Jonathan thought he could reach the Munsonville store, some three miles distant, and be home in plenty of time before nightfall as it was a journey he had undertaken many times in the past. And so he set out on a rugged trail through the woods *"to do some trading."*

The light snow fall quickly changed to a blizzard, however, intensifying as he progressed. Knee-high drifts formed before he was able to make his way back. The proprietors of the small country store remembered later that Jonathan had reached them and, as quoted in a newspaper article from the New Hampshire Sentinel of 1877, *"after completing his business started for home in the midst of the storm"* with the family's groceries and mail. The temperature dipped and the wind-driven snow increased. With visibility dropping, it became difficult for Jonathan to see if he was still heading in the right direction. Following the river toward home, he crossed the ice at one point and climbed the bank on the other side. With less than a mile to go, Jonathan wandered off the path and, succumbing either to exhaustion or hypothermia, sat down under a large maple tree to rest. He never got back up.

When the weather cleared the next morning, Jonathan's family and men from the town began searching for him. They followed the trail he would have taken but found no trace of him. Elsie's diary mentions that *"40 men are hunting for my father."* For a week they searched, and found only the *"pail and oil can"* he left beside the trail.

Three months later, on March 25, 1877, as the winter snows began to melt, Jonathan's body was found *"within a few rods of where he left his can and pail."* The newspaper article reported, *"The body was in a good state of preservation, embedded in snow, with no indications that it had in any way been disturbed in its icy surroundings for the three months since his death."* His gravestone in the Munsonville,

New Hampshire, cemetery recounts the tale of his tragic death: *"He perished of cold by the wayside in trying to reach his home. Fo(u)nd Mar.25, 1877, died Dec. 29, 1876."* (See "Stoddard History in Verse" in Perley's Poetry)

Stoddard Center in 1901
Courtesy of Historical Society of Cheshire County

Picture of Rosina Delight Richardson Wood which hung
on Perley's wall for almost 100 years
Rosina was born in 1833 - Died in 1878

Perley's barn built around 1792
Courtesy of Quentin White

Perley's house in Stoddard
Built by Danforth Taylor in 1801
Courtesy of Quentin White

Jonathan Harvey Whittier
Perley's grandfather
Born April 30, 1818 - Died December 29, 1876

Jonathan H. Whittier gravestone in Munsonville, NH cemetery

Chapter Two
Elsie Jane

Perley's mother, Elsie Jane Whittier, was only sixteen years old when her father died. Suddenly, the care of the 130-acre homestead was left to Jonathan's fifty year old widow, Mary, and her two daughters, Elsie Jane and Lydia May. (The oldest daughter, Almina Mahala, had already married and moved to a farm of her own). Possessing much stronger determination and grit than her mother and younger sister, Elsie Jane knew it would be up to her to take over the majority of the duties caring for the farm if her family was to survive. This sense of responsibility carried with it a feeling of love for and pride in the land, a commitment that would stay with Elsie Jane for the next sixty-eight years (and ultimately pass on to her future son, Perley). With the help of neighbors and hired men, Elsie Jane, her mom and sister were able to manage the farm.

Elsie Jane had the potential to be a very attractive woman with clear, smooth skin, high cheekbones, large penetrating eyes, straight teeth and thick wavy brown hair. Had she a more approachable personality, this combination might have made a very inviting package. But nothing soft and feminine greeted those that met Elsie Jane. Though not physically intimidating, Elsie Jane could cause anyone to wither before her formidable countenance. Thin lips, pursed tightly together, gave her face a stern and solemn demeanor which was accentuated by wearing her hair pulled back in a severe bun. Elsie Jane's olive-tone skin darkened easily from time spent working outdoors. She resembled a proud Indian woman when she stood, ramrod straight, presiding over her land and contemplating the never ending list of chores that needed to be done.

In 1878, eighteen-year old Elsie Jane Whittier married an older man by the name of William Darling. It was the only time in her life she lived away from her home place. The marriage only lasted long enough to produce two daughters, whom Elsie named Festina and Myrtie. Through correspondence with Mr. Darling at the time, it seems likely that Elsie Jane left him because of some kind of abuse. In begging her to come back, Mr. Darling wrote: *"Though I may have been unkind in the past, I will prove to you I will make up for it in the future."* Elsie instead chose to move with her two daughters back to the home she loved and had grown up in next to Taylor Pond.

At that time, Elsie's mother, Mary, had already moved away from the family homestead. She preferred to stay in Hillsboro, a town nearby, in order to live an easier life than that of farming. She turned the land and buildings over to her daughters and, in time, Elsie Jane bought out the interests of her two sisters.

Life must not have been easy for a single mother and two young children living so far away from the nearest neighbors. Any trip to buy needed supplies became an all day ordeal as Elsie loaded her daughters onto the horse and wagon to make the several mile journey over bad roads. However, Elsie Jane seemed to find strength and purpose in hard work. Though exhausted at the end of each day, she was content with the direction that her life was taking.

Six years passed quickly as Elsie Jane worked from morning until night to manage her land. Content to be alone with her daughters at first, Elsie's isolation finally led her to be interested when, in 1884, a man by the name of Daniel Swett rented a house a few miles beyond her farm. Gossip at the time was that Daniel's initial intention was to court the Widow Whittier, Elsie's mother. But, once he met Elsie Jane and perhaps realized she had taken ownership of the family homestead, he decided he would pursue her to be his bride. Daniel was forty-seven when he proposed to Elsie Jane, who was just twenty-six. It was to be Daniel's third marriage.

"Dan Swett was a character in his time in that small community," an aged acquaintance recalled, *"Elsie Jane was quite a contrast to Dan who was of slight stature, with twinkling blue eyes, and a pink and white complexion. He had a sunny, happy disposition."* Daniel may have been able to turn on the charm when necessary but some people said the "sunny, happy disposition" came out of a bottle and could easily turn dark at the slightest provocation.

In later years, Perley would say of his ancestors, *"Doubtless the Swetts got out of England one jump ahead of the hangman's noose."* What basis he had for such a comment is not known but it seems likely he suspected his father was not of the same moral fiber that Elsie Jane had inherited from her Quaker ancestors. Prevailing opinion in the town seemed to be that Daniel was less than ambitious. This was a notion that would follow Dan until the day he died thirty-eight years later at the age of eighty-three. When his body was being transported to his gravesite a neighbor was heard to mutter, *"That's probably the fastest ol' Dan has ever moved."*

It would certainly be understandable that Elsie Jane felt the need for a man to help her care for her home and two young daughters. They had been alone too long and isolated as they were Elsie Jane may have worried there would be few prospects for marriage in her future. Though Daniel Swett *"came with nothing but the clothes on his back,"* as Perley later recalled, Elsie Jane agreed to marry him.

The next year, Elsie Jane and Daniel began expanding their family with the birth of their daughter, Nora May. Two years later, on February 6, 1888, Perley Edwin Swett came into the world "just before the Blizzard of '88." This tremendous snowstorm wreaked havoc during the month of March. The blizzard concentrated its fury on New York City and the entire East Coast, bringing every horse car, cable car, and elevated train to a halt. In Pittsfield, Massachusetts the main street was buried under twenty feet of drifting snow. Some houses were completely covered. Fierce winds piled up forty foot drifts. Forty to fifty inches of snow fell throughout New England from Connecticut to Maine. Two hundred people lost their lives. It would take weeks for the families in rural New Hampshire to dig their way out and resume normal lives.

Dora Bumford had the unfortunate distinction of being one of those two hundred who died during "the Blizzard of '88." Adora "Dora" Cunningham was born in Unity, New Hampshire in 1862. She married Arthur Bumford in Hillsborough in 1884. The couple soon moved to Stoddard where Arthur took over operations of the sawmill that had likely been a home to Rosina Richardson Wood. The sawmill was now known as "Woods Mill." On March 13, just five weeks after Perley was born a mile up the road, 24-year-old Dora died in the midst of the now famous blizzard. Because of the huge snowdrifts, her body could not be removed from the mill area and Dora was buried in a sandbank near the mill house. Though it seems likely this makeshift grave was meant to be only temporary, Dora remained buried there for thirty years...until 1928 when the new owner of the property felt a proper burial was in order.

Perley

In contrast to her other children, and perhaps as an omen for the life he would lead, Perley's was a difficult birth. And as a result, Elsie Jane was confined to her bed during the rest of that long, hard winter. In a letter that Elsie's mother, Mary, wrote to her oldest daughter, Almina, she said that, *"Elsie can't get up to save her life but she don't get so discouraged as I should. You know she is blessed with great fortitude and good constitution."*

At the age of fifty, Daniel was relieved to finally have a son to carry on his family name. But it was Elsie Jane who was the most enamored of her first male child. She named him after her grandfather, Perley Andrews, and formed a closeness to him that she never felt with her other children. As a result, Elsie Jane spoiled and over-protected Perley as he grew. Throughout his whole life, in her eyes, Perley would do no wrong. Perhaps she sensed that of all her children he would be the one who would take over her farm someday, loving and cherishing her land and home as much as she did.

Accustomed to Elsie Jane being in charge of the household and many of the day to day chores of running the farm, it was difficult for the family to have her bedridden after Perley's birth. And being forced to lie in bed was no easier for Elsie Jane. She was used to hard work and took pride in managing her home and family. The girls, especially Elsie Jane's two oldest daughters, who Daniel sometimes referred to as "those damn monkeys," suffered from not having Elsie Jane available to run interference between them and their stepfather. In later years Daniel's own sister wrote Elsie a letter voicing her sympathy, *"It always made me feel so bad to have him so ugly to you and the children. I did pity them so."*

Clearly, life with Daniel had not turned out as Elsie Jane had hoped. Having been raised in a family of teetotalers, Elsie Jane was unprepared to deal with Daniel's drinking. His constant verbal attacks and mood swings kept the family walking on eggshells when he was tippling. He was slowly undermining Elsie Jane's authority and self-confidence. Though not a physical beating, it was having the same wearing effect. Elsie was becoming quiet and withdrawn, allowing Daniel to have the final say in all matters. She found it easier than arguing with him. Elsie's mother, Mary, stayed with the Swett family to help during Elsie's confinement but this gave Daniel even more to rant and rave about. In one fit of anger, he kicked over the small wood pile stacked in Mary's room and screamed and swore at his mother-in-law, calling her *"a beggar that has to be fed."*

Not surprisingly, Mary did not think very highly of Daniel. *"It was something new,"* complained Mary, *"in all the years we have lived there, to see such a destitute house."* She went on to say that Daniel *"did not get up a good wood pile for the first of winter"* and so he was forced to take the oxen out in the deep snow to forage for more. Food for the family was also at an all time low: *"not raising enough grain he* [Daniel] *got out of meat and we had to cut potatoes three times a day and fed the hens on them as well and now not a potato to eat."* Mary subsequently wrote in a letter that she, *"told Elsie I didn't pity him much, I never was used to such 'shifflessness'."*

The family endured that long, difficult winter (*"The oldest people never see such a time"*) with Elsie finally returning to robust health and Perley growing into a healthy, though somewhat diminutive boy. Having three older sisters did not make life easy for Perley. His personality was in sharp contrast to theirs. They were boisterous and outgoing. Perley was quiet and sensitive. The girls took advantage of this and their brother's smaller size, bossing him about and treating him as their plaything, a life-sized doll. This teasing and taunting, good natured as it might have been, did not sit well with Perley whose only means of defense was to run to his mother. And thus began a pattern of behavior, an unusually strong mother-son protectiveness, that would last for much of Perley's life.

Many years later, when Nora was approaching the age of fifty, she addressed this issue in a letter she wrote to her mother. *"Perley should be caring for you now instead of heaping all his troubles on you. You have done so much for him. But he always did come to you for protection when he could not have his own way. I always thought, and still believe, that if you had taken him over your knee and paddled him in good shape and told him to fight his own battles it would have made more of a man of him. But those times Myrtie and I used to dress him up in girls clothes and tease him are some of the happy memories of my childhood. We were speaking of it recently when Myrtie was on her vacation and we both thought we could do it again. How he would kick and strike. Poor Perley."*

When Perley was three years old, another son, Luman Frederick, was born to Elsie Jane and Daniel. Perley was thrilled; he would finally have an ally against his sisters. However, Luman died within a few months, leaving Perley devastated by the loss. The baby was buried in an unmarked grave on the family farm. Perley always felt a deep connection to this little brother, perhaps a contributing factor to his wanting to be buried in his company in later life.

Three more children, Ella, Walter and Martin, were born to Elsie Jane and Daniel over the next few years. All the children were born at home, the last son in 1901 when Elsie was forty-one.

The Swett family now totaled nine, though by the time the youngest were born Elsie Jane's oldest daughters were already working for and living with other families. The small house was bursting at the seams but no one expected creature comforts. All they had ever known was a meager existence.

Though caring for a house and seven children was more than enough for any one woman to handle, Elsie's passion was to be outdoors. Having been something of a tomboy, she preferred working in the fields to being captive in a hot, stuffy kitchen. Haying, maple sugaring, planting and caring for the gardens, harvesting fruit, berries and vegetables...all beckoned to Elsie Jane. Yet necessity also brought her inside to do 'woman's' work. For Daniel contributed little to the household chores.

Elsie Jane was an animal lover and had many as pets both domestic and wild. These included a tame crow trained to eat bread from her hand; a family of foxes which lived under the old barn and came out to play when she sat near and tossed them scraps of food; an injured squirrel that Elsie nursed back to health and which then took up residence in the house. The children were always bringing wounded animals home for Elsie Jane to doctor. *"I have nine baby ducks that lost their mother,"* she wrote to her sister, *"They are about a week old. They get in the old sink under the eaves and swim and are real cute."* The menagerie was complemented by an assortment of cats and dogs.

All the livestock were regarded as members of the family. Elsie always named the cows and horses and it was a great cause for sadness if a family pet ever had to be "put down." *"Ranger has been a good, dear, faithful friend to me for nearly twelve years,"* wrote Elsie Jane about her horse, *"but he had lost the use of his legs so bad I thought best to have him put away."*

Actual cash money was a rare commodity for the family and Elsie Jane did all she could to help earn it. She made trips into the city of Keene, about ten miles away, every other week. She loaded up her wagon with vegetables, butter she had churned, ("*I sell about 10 ½ pounds a trip*") maple syrup or whatever fruit or berries might have been in season. "*I picked nineteen quarts of blueberries.*" She wrote in her journal, "*I got 15 cents a quart for some and twelve cents for the rest.*" She visited any stores or restaurants willing to buy her wares, and returned home quite disappointed if unable to make any sales.

In her later years, after Daniel passed away, Elsie Jane became a figure of curiosity, and even ridicule, to the townspeople as she trundled along in her horse and wagon, dressed in an old-fashioned, tattered coat which covered the long skirts she wore even in summer. Wisps of gray hair flew about her face, escaping from the bun she still wore and the sunbonnet that topped it. Her ensemble was completed by Daniel's oversized galoshes which she wore over her shoes as protection from puddles or mud.

Sitting under the large umbrella Perley had tied to the wagon, she bounced along the roads, holding a conversation with "Jerry," "Dandy," "Buster" or whichever was the current family horse delegated to pull the wagon. (That same umbrella caused Perley to have a narrow escape when it was hit by lightning while he traveled home from town. "*When I 'came to life' the horse was still down, but ready to get up and be on the way home with grain and groceries.*" Perley recalled that this episode "*Weakened my eyes for several days as well as the right side of my face feeling queer. Perhaps the nearest I ever came to Heaven, or the other place, if Saint Peter refused me admittance past the gates.*")

Elsie Jane enjoyed her forays into Keene but it was always a relief to be back home. The trip could be arduous for both human and beast and her first concern was that her equine friend was well taken care of. "*Dandy had hurt his right hind leg,*" she explained in a letter to a relative. "*It was badly swollen from his body to his hoof. I used up a bottle of*

Sloan's liniment on it and one of Minard's, then I put on beef brine and it begun to be better."

Throughout her long life, Elsie Jane would remain devoted to Perley. She worked tirelessly on his behalf, contributing her labor to help sustain the family farm with the intention of passing it along to her eldest son. And through all the trials and tribulations that would beset Perley, Elsie Jane would remain his staunchest - and at times only - defender. But in the end, she could not protect him from himself...and Perley would prove to be his own worst enemy.

Elsie Jane Whittier and Daniel Edwin Swett
Perley's parents

L-R: Myrtie Darling, Perley about two years old,
Festina Darling and Nora May Swett
Taken around 1890

Chapter Three
Growing up

Friday, January 1st, 1904, dawned cold and cloudy. The temperature was only eight degrees above zero. It was snowing lightly with a strong westerly wind. We know this now, over one hundred years later, because Perley kept detailed daily journals throughout most of his life. He began his first one in 1904 when he was just fifteen years old. Though the family seldom exchanged gifts, Perley's sister Nora had given him a diary the previous Christmas.

[Author's Note: A daily journal can tell us a lot about the time in which it was written. In Perley's case it tells us not simply *what* happened but suggests vividly what life was like *when* it happened. This has allowed me to pick and choose from his journal entries to paint a picture of Perley's growing-up years, one hundred years ago, shaping the man he would become.]

Though Daniel chose to avoid hard work whenever possible, he did not like to see his children idle. There were always more chores to be done than time available in the day and he expected them to keep busy. Perley and his siblings had very little time for relaxation and fun. So Perley enjoyed the few minutes of peace and quiet he was allowed at the end of every day to write in his journal. It became a habit which stayed with him almost until the day he died.

GROWING UP

Perley began that first diary entry, and each new page, with a quick synopsis of the weather. Anyone who kept a journal in those days seemed to think it was necessary to record for posterity the atmospheric conditions.

The rich record Perley preserved of his life growing up shows a farm family busy with chores at home as might be expected. But the farm at the beginning of the 20th century was also very much a part of a more populous extended neighborhood. It wasn't uncommon to have friends and neighbors, even strangers, stopping by each day as they passed through the area, sometimes staying for a meal or overnight. Evidence of this neighborhood activity is given in Perley's journal entry of January 12th, 1904. With the temperature only reaching sixteen degrees above zero, Perley wrote: *"Tom Hastings and George Davis stopped here; Byron Holt and Martin Barret stopped here, too. Lillian and Charlie came up here after a lb. of butter. Papa went over to Mr. Pepper's; Mama went over to Mrs. Dyer's. Everett came over here, he is going to Keene tomorrow. I went over there with a sleigh twice. Ella & Walter & Martin* [Perley's siblings] *went too. I went over after supper to get a letter."* This amount of daily activity seemed to be quite common. Many days were filled with neighbors visiting or the Swetts calling on friends.

Though Perley's neighborhood was still very rural, the well-traveled road which passed by their house had been a stage coach route for many years, connecting the two small towns of Sullivan and Stoddard. The road then and certainly now, was much better suited for a horse and wagon than the coming of the automobile.

Perley's days on the farm started early. Daily labor was repeated in the same sequence from year to year and revolved around the seasons. All the children had chores for which they alone were responsible. Perley raised chickens. Separated into two groups, he referred to them in his journal as his "barn hens" and, curiously, "these hens." Each day he recorded how many eggs they respectively laid. Though not very productive in the winter, by spring the "barn hens" had laid 1,027 eggs for the month of April and "these hens" laid 1,239.

Often neighbors carried the eggs to town to sell. *"Everett Dyer took seventy-nine dozen eggs to carry to Keene"* where they would sell for thirty cents a dozen. Sometimes Perley loaded up the wagon, a hand sled or simply sacks on his back with eggs or other goods the farm had produced. Following the same fateful path his grandfather had taken, Perley traveled the three miles to the Munsonville store where the produce was traded for grain or other needed supplies.

Daniel helped Perley build a *"set-house to shut the setting hens in."* When Perley said he *"set a hen to the barn today"* it meant he put a hen on a nest of eggs in an enclosed area so it would be forced to sit on the eggs keeping them warm until they hatched. Neighbors would buy not only the eggs but the chicks themselves. *"Mr. Blood came over and bought a hen and eight chickens for a dollar. We took them off the nest; they had just hatched."*

The chickens, especially the "sick" ones (though what they were sick with is never made clear) were killed for meat for the family. Raptors were sometimes a nuisance when raising chicks so if a dead chicken was found Perley observed that, *"Papa set a trap on it for a hawk."*

January was a particularly cold month in 1904 although the accuracy of Perley's meteorological reporting may be questioned. He wrote that on *"the fourth of this month it was over fifty below in Keene."* It seems the family was worried that the year ahead was going to continue to be a cold one. Perley wrote that *"Paul* [Dyer] *said yesterday that someone told him there was a planet between the sun and earth, and it was going to be a cold summer. It was in 1816 that we had one before; there was snow every month in the year. Papa's father remembered it."*

The year 1816 was indeed the "year without a summer." A saved newspaper article of the time described it as *"the coldest ever known in this latitude; frost and ice were common. Almost every green thing was killed; fruit nearly all destroyed."* A large snowstorm in June resulted in many human deaths. Historians now ascribe the bad weather and loss of crops to volcanic activity, saying this phenomenon was *"a primary motivation for the western movement and rapid settlement of the American Midwest."* It is also what forced author, Mary Shelley, and friends to stay indoors for much of their Swiss holiday. Out of boredom, they decided to have a contest to see who could write the scariest story. The result was Shelley's classic, *Frankenstein*.

There were bushels of stored fruits and vegetables kept in the basement under the house. With no electric refrigeration, the cellar was the only place foods could be preserved at a cool temperature both winter and summer. If any produce froze it would quickly rot when it thawed. Every few weeks Elsie Jane or one of the kids would pick through the bins of fruits and vegetables and throw out any rotten ones so they would not contaminate the rest.

Several times each winter Daniel had to make a fire on the dirt floor in the basement under the house to keep the produce and foods in canning jars from freezing. But this was not always successful. Perley recorded that on February 10th his father miscalculated and the *"milk in the cupboard froze solid and the cream jar froze to the cellar bottom."*

Everyone in the neighborhood was constantly on the alert for a way to make a few dollars. No job was considered too menial. For anyone who was fortunate enough to own land, logging it off was an obvious way to earn money. On February 27th Perley wrote that *"Papa went down to the mill. Harry Wilson was there. Papa has sold him 22,276 feet of old growth timber, at $3.50 a thousand, they finished measuring it today."* Because lumbering was hard and dangerous and required teams of horses or oxen to haul the logs to a sawmill, it was much simpler to sell the trees to lumber companies which would then send in their own experienced and well-equipped teams.

Winter was the best time of the year to drag the logs out of the woods, with the ground covered in snow and the roads frozen. In warmer weather the mud could make it nearly impossible to operate. Perley mentioned seeing the teams going by his house, *"Four chair shop teams were drawing lumber today; three of Hasting's teams are drawing lumber past here. Joe Waldron was going after logs with his steers."*

Though Perley was only a young teenager, he and Daniel often filled in when needed at the Wood's Mill a mile south of their farm, sawing and planing the logs into lumber. The work was sporadic, depending on the weather and whether the machinery was operating on any given day.

Spring was a welcome relief after a long, hard winter. With the advent of warmer days but cold nights, the sap from the maple trees started running. Many farm families used maple sugar in place of store bought cane sugar for all of their sweetening needs. Not only was it cheaper, it had become a New England tradition. Because most of the cane sugar was produced in the southern states, many northern families had stopped using it during the Civil War (1861-1865) as a protest. Poorer families, like Perley's, stuck with maple sugaring to provide a cheaper source of sweetener for their foods. As Perley's journal reported, *"Today we set out enough sap buckets to make 75 in all."* As the pails filled, Perley and his siblings would take the horse and wagon and once or twice a day, depending on how fast it was running, collect the sap. Going from tree to tree, they'd transfer the buckets of sap into larger containers on the wagon and then hauled it back to the "boiling place." Undoubtedly one of the sheds was set up for that use as the family could not afford to build a 'sugar house' specifically for that seasonal purpose.

During the height of the sugaring season, Perley and his family would boil syrup every day in order to keep up with the sap run. *"The sap runs good now,"* Perley said on March 31st when they made over three gallons of syrup and *"a little over four pails of soft sugar, about twenty-eight pounds."*

Having little or no cash, farm families resorted to manufacturer's premiums for household items. Perley recorded on April 16 that he *"wrote a letter to Washburn-Crosby Co, Minneapolis, Minn.* [which later was to become General Mills] *I am going to send a gold medal flour trade mark and an advertisement and they will send me a jack-knife."* The next day Elsie Jane wrote to the same company for a knife for Perley's younger sister, Ella. Also Perley wrote that *"Papa is going to send fifty Burr Oak tobacco tags to Harry Weissinger Tobacco Co., Louisville, Ky. to get a knife."*

Most clothes the children wore were homemade or hand-me-downs given to them by relatives and friends. As the oldest outgrew them, the clothes were passed down to younger brothers and sisters. On rare occasions Perley was able to buy something brand new, such as the time he went to Munsonville and *"got a pair of Congress shoes for seventy-five cents."* Congress shoes were the height of fashion for a gentleman as early as the mid 1800s. When elastic was invented, shoes were one of it's first uses. Congress shoes were ankle high with elastic gussets in the sides. They may not have been much use doing chores but Perley felt quite dashing with them on.

As spring neared, it was time to prepare the gardens for planting. The horse was hooked up to a 'side-hill' or swivel plow. This was a walking plow, which meant someone had to walk behind to steady it and keep it digging in a straight line. There were no moving or mechanical parts, just a sharp, curved steel blade to dig and turn the earth as the 'plowman' applied steady pressure on the handles. These tools worked particularly well in the stony and irregular ground of the New Hampshire countryside. Perley's younger siblings had the job of picking out the stones that continually popped to the surface from plowing...and also collecting the uncovered earthworms which were saved for fishing trips to the pond or to be sold to neighbors.

Once the ground was plowed, the gardens were planted. This was usually done around Memorial Day after all threat of frost was over. It also is the time when millions of ravenous black flies hatch. Anyone living in the New Hampshire countryside, especially near brooks or slow-moving streams, knows how easily these swarms of black flies can interrupt outdoor chores and send one beating a hasty retreat indoors. *"I believe no other area in this part of the USA is quite as bad as this section of Stoddard,"* Perley would recall in his later years, *"Even the goats stay in the barn when black flies are in season."*

Because the Swett family lived year-round on the crops they raised, several acres of different vegetables had to be planted. Usually it took two to three weeks to put all the crops into the ground. At that critical time of year, neighbors played a vital role in helping each other with the planting. On May 27th Perley recorded that *"Frank Fifield came over and planted a piece* [patch] *of corn with his machine."*

An amazing variety of fruits and berries, either cultivated or wild, were picked to be consumed at home or sold. Elsie Jane and the children spent the summers into the fall picking raspberries, blueberries, blackberries, strawberries, currants, pears, plums, grapes and many different kinds of apples.

Some of the apples were turned into cider and vinegar which they sold. Even catnip was raised and sold. Everything that grew was used. Nothing was wasted.

When a vegetable was in season and abundant, it was not uncommon to have that vegetable for every meal. Perley mentions in his journal, *"We had some green peas this morning for breakfast."* It was a good year for squashes and pumpkins also, and the family ended up with over one hundred of them. There were enough to eat and to sell: *"Mr. Pepper bought two hundred lbs. of squashes here for two dollars."* Fifty bushels of potatoes and twenty barrels of apples were harvested but, unfortunately, *"the frost spoilt all the grapes, except some wild ones that had got ripe."*

Calves born on the farm were usually sold. Cows were used for milk and meat. From the cream the family made their own butter. To do this they first needed to take the cream out of the milk. Elsie Jane used a machine called a "separator." (For many years cream was separated from the milk by the gravity method: pans were filled with milk and allowed to sit until the cream rose to the top. This primitive method was not only time-consuming, it allowed bacteria to form. With the invention of the "separator," a machine which basically spun the milk out of the cream, hours or even days of waiting were saved.) Once enough cream had been collected, it was put into a butter churn which, when continuously agitated, separated the fats from the liquid. (Butter is essentially the fat component of milk.) Elsie Jane would then sell the surplus butter she made to neighbors.

The tall grass in the fields was cut by hand with a scythe, raked up and thrown into a wagon to be hauled to the barn. Neighbors often pooled their efforts to get the hay in quickly before it could rain. No fancy bailing machines were used. In later years Daniel was able to acquire a used horse-drawn "mowing machine" which cut the hay much more quickly though it was still hand-raked.

A lot of bartering took place in the neighborhood. When a family moved away they would have an auction to sell off what they couldn't bring with them, much the same as modern day yard sales. Perley and his family acquired most of their needed equipment and tools that way.

Other odd jobs were done for whatever income could be brought in. Daniel would sharpen saw blades for neighbors in exchange for some favor. Family records show that on one occasion he sold a skunk skin to a passerby for a quarter. Perley wrote that they sold a visiting "Ragman" *"two dollars worth of rags, rubber and lead."* A "ragman" collected such items for resale to others, often to use in making new products. Rags, for example, were used to make paper.

The children would go barefoot as much as possible to save wear and tear on their shoes. The town actually paid Daniel five dollars toward shoe leather each year so the children could attend school. Typically, there were several small schools in each town to allow easy access; many children really did walk several miles 'uphill both ways' to reach their schools. The teachers often were young girls who had just finished their own schooling and took on the role of teaching their younger charges. Several times Perley mentions that different teachers came to spend the night. *"The teacher, Miss Anna B. Stoddard, came home with us and stayed over night. She went back this morning."* This was part of their pay, to be fed and housed by parents of their students. Also, it was a way for these young teachers to get to know their student's family situations.

Beginning with his early years in grammar school, Perley showed promise of a quick mind. He enjoyed school and was especially good at geography and writing. But by the time he was fifteen he was no longer attending the neighborhood school; he was needed at home. His parents felt he could make better use of his time by working than by attending school. He did sometimes fill in as teacher to his younger siblings when they were unable to attend classes or there was no teacher available. The town paid a small stipend to Perley for doing this.

Still, Perley never lost his love for books and reading and often relied on relatives and neighbors for reading material. Knowing his penchant for learning, friends would save old newspapers, magazines and books to give to Perley when they saw him.

Daniel never did understand Perley's interest in learning about the world around him. As far as Daniel was concerned, all Perley needed to know was what took place on the farm. Unfortunately this was one instance when Elsie Jane agreed with Daniel. Caring for the farm and land was her highest priority, next to her children, and she didn't want to encourage any curiosity that might lead her favorite son to leave it some day. Like the dutiful son he was, Perley accepted this parental opinion and, ultimately, made it his own.

Though Perley gave up his chance to advance his education without a fight, he never wished to show ignorance. One of the most well-used gifts he ever received was a Webster's Dictionary. He checked his spelling constantly, especially later in life when he wrote letters and poetry to friends. To save money, he even developed his own style of "legalese" for documents and correspondence that would normally be handled by lawyers. Despite his lack of formal education, Perley would become quite active, though seldom successful, as his own legal counsel.

Because of the distance and difficulty of getting the whole family to services on Sunday, church and religion did not seem to play a big part in Perley's life. Indeed, the only time Perley mentions going to church was to *"eat a bean supper."*

Christmas and most holidays passed by with hardly a mention in Perley's journals. The only form of celebration Perley mentioned for his sixteenth birthday was that *"Mamma made the last two squashes into pies."* However, Thanksgiving was one holiday the family did celebrate. It became tradition for Elsie Jane to prepare a large family feast for Thanksgiving. She loved to gather her children and later grandchildren around the big kitchen table. The menu included such delicacies as venison, wild turkey, and fish. Rabbits, squirrels and other small animals were made into stews. It was said that Elsie Jane could make a pretty decent hedgehog pie! Although Thanksgiving was a time for celebration, attendees were expected to mind their manners. Elva Swett Frazier remembers Thanksgiving Dinner at her grandmother's house. *"Grammy Swett was kind but stern."* She said, *"You always knew you had to sit quietly and eat your meal."*

Daniel was not particularly close to his children as they grew. Many times he went his own way, leaving Elsie Jane in charge of their care and upbringing. Considering himself the head of the household, though, Daniel expected compliance not only from his children but also his wife. To keep some harmony in the family, Elsie Jane seemed willing to accept that her place was in submission to her husband.

Perley would not have learned exceptional parenting or marriage skills from his father. Though he did not like the way Daniel treated his mother or the family, Perley had no other father figure to compare him to and so grew up thinking that this was the way a father ran the family. Years later this way of thinking did not serve him well in dealing with his own marriage to a more determined wife.

GROWING UP

Daniel and Elsie raised their children as old fashioned, straight-laced disciplinarians. Perley grew up with a very clear impression of what was expected of him. Either something was right or it was wrong; there were no grey areas. Therefore, it was a jolt to Perley as he aged to realize that not everyone thought the way he did.

The world in which he was raised in rural Stoddard was extremely narrow in terms of life experiences and Perley's view of that world was influenced only by friends and neighbors much like his own family. With no television or radio and only an occasional newspaper to bring in news of the outside world, Perley was shielded from the realities of life, some harsher than others. It was with a certain amount of incredulity that he faced his first experience with dishonesty. *"I fed a tramp Sunday,"* he wrote in one of his journals in 1909, *"and today I discovered the loss of a pair of good mittens. It is the first thing I ever lost that way, also the first tramp I ever fed."* Perley was almost twenty-one at the time when the first seeds of distrust of his fellow man began to grow.

In later years, in a letter Elsie Jane wrote to a court judge defending Perley, she told how at the age of six Perley said he was going to work hard and save all the money he earned because *"more than anything else when I become a man I want to buy a farm of my own."* This was his plan, and starting at a very young age he worked tirelessly to achieve it. *"One Friday night as Perley was coming by the Barker place,"* Elsie Jane recalled, *"Mr. Charlie Wellman said to him, 'I will give you a dollar if you will come over and dig potatoes for me tomorrow.' Perley told him he would. He came home, much pleased with the chance to earn money and he worked all that fall digging potatoes and picking apples. He also picked berries and other things to earn money."*

Perley

As a teenager, Perley worked odd jobs for neighbors, putting in ten to twelve hour days and receiving $1.00 a day for his labors. When Perley was eighteen he did as many young adults, including his sisters before him, had done. He hired out as an extra hand at wealthier farms. Most of these young employees lived with their employers, being accepted and treated as one of the family. Chores ranged from caring for the chickens, cattle and other livestock to planting and tending the garden, haying, chopping wood and running errands. Occasionally Perley would have to play the role of baby-sitter, taking the children to school and watching over them after school. No "job description" limited his duties. As a young live-in worker, Perley did whatever was needed by his host family.

Perley continued in this type of work for the next two years. Having very little to spend his money on and wanting to build a healthy bank account, it didn't take long before Perley could consider buying a farm of his own.

In 1909, when Perley was turning twenty-one, Charlie Tuttle's farm, known as the "Old Hastings Place," just two miles down the road from his parent's home came up for sale. This was the opportunity Perley had been dreaming of. Everything was falling neatly into place just as he always planned. Perley purchased the house along with 124 acres of land. He was ready to take his meager belongings and move out on his own. There was only one problem: it would be impossible to do all the work necessary to take care of his new farm alone, and hiring help was too costly. Perley might ask for assistance from his family but his parents were getting old and needed their remaining children, who were still living at home, to help them.

There was only one solution to his dilemma. Perley needed to start his own family. Perley needed a wife!

L-R: Mary Andrews Whittier, Elsie Jane holding Walter, Myrtie Darling in doorway, Perley, Festina Darling holding cat, Nora, Ella and Daniel Swett

Sample of Perley's journal entry from July, 1904

Chapter Four
A Marriage of Hope

Perley's new farm was situated just over the town line in Sullivan, New Hampshire. The "Old Hastings Place" had 124 acres, fifteen of which were prime, open fields ideal for planting crops. The asking price was $700. Perley had $500 in the bank. His mother willingly loaned him the remaining money, which he soon paid back.

By the time Perley purchased this land, it had been a farm for almost one hundred years. Benjamin Hastings, a Revolutionary War veteran, had bought the property in 1806 and lived there with his son in the original house. Deciding to build new, they bought an old house nearby and used the materials from that to build their "new" house in 1843. Hastings was a man of eighty at the time. They lived there for several years but eventually the farm was sold to Charles Howard, a Civil War veteran and grandson to Danforth and Tabitha Taylor. Mr. Howard owned the homestead for eighteen years before selling it to the lumber business of Goodnow and Hubbard for the valuable timber on the property. Finally, Charles Tuttle bought the house for his family in 1907, owning it only two years before he turned it over to Perley, *"along with a wagon, horse rake, plank, brooder, horse machine and other small things."*

Perley's house was a shingled two-story, central chimney structure with nine windows at the front to take advantage of a countryside view. On the main floor were four large rooms, a kitchen with a large brick oven, a pantry and three fireplaces. Upstairs there were two more fireplaces and a "dance hall" across the front of the house. At one time school was kept there.

There is nothing left today to show that a proud house stood there for more than a century and was home to a succession of families. At the time Perley bought it, the house must have seemed like a mansion compared to the home in which he'd grown up. There were several out-buildings, including a 20x40' ell used as a woodshed and a 100 foot long barn that set back from the house. Ultimately, a freak tornado would pass through the area in 1920 and blow the barn to rubble.

Under the main part of the house a cellar had been hand dug. A "never failing" spring across the road promised a constant supply of water. Abundant wild blueberry bushes kept Perley supplied with "berry money" for many years to come. Lilacs, roses, snowball and June Pink bushes added color to the property. There were also many apple and sugar maple trees. Perley's new home was potentially sustainable...if enough hands could be found to work it.

Perley immediately started increasing his land holdings by acquiring a wood lot of thirty-five acres bordering his property. He now owned 159 acres with a property tax of just $17.00 a year. One horse, three cows and some chickens (no goats!) made up his livestock. Perley was on his way to becoming one of the largest land holders in town. Grand visions of being a wealthy land baron filled his head.

Perley worked his farm for the next two years by himself. Family and neighbors offered to help when they could. On June 4, 1909, Perley wrote in his diary that, *"Dunbar's team came to plow for me, mother got 5 bushels of potatoes for me, Father came over and helped some and Walter and Martin* [brothers] *stayed tonight and helped plant some."* He furnished his new home with items bought at auctions and increased his livestock in trades with neighbors. *"I traded my Holstein cow to Bert Currier,"* Perley wrote in his journal, *"for a large white horse named Prince."*

There wasn't much free time to think about anything else but when Perley finally crawled into bed at night, exhausted from his never-ending chores, he felt something was missing. Though at first relishing the peace and quiet of his new home, he found himself wishing for companionship, even the commotion of a large family and knew his house was too big for just one person. Also, even working from sunrise to sunset there was still no way he could handle all the work necessary to maintain his farm the way he wanted.

Meeting and courting a potential partner was not going to be easy, tied down as Perley was to farm work and with few girls his age in the neighborhood. Though a handsome young man, he had never even had a girlfriend. But Perley was a romantic at heart, already dabbling in poetry:

*"I dream of loving arms around me, and I so much want sweet kisses too;
And I hope ere many more years pass, this dream will come to me true."*

Being such an innocent and possessing a highly idealized view of what he considered to be the perfect wife, Perley fantasized about the flawless woman he would meet and marry. In so doing he would be setting himself up for a fall.

Coincidentally, not too far away there seemed a very likely candidate who was also in the process of looking for a spouse. Helen Eva Whitney was living in Antrim, New Hampshire, ten miles east of Sullivan. She and Perley were already slightly acquainted and had been keeping in touch through infrequent letters over the years. They had been neighbors when both were very young when Helen's family had rented a home nearby in Stoddard. When she moved away, Helen gave Perley his first kiss, much to his chagrin but to the delight of his older sisters who continued to tease him about it for many years to come.

As Perley later recalled, *"The party I married lived in this section when young, and kissed me goodbye when leaving at the age of five. I do not remember it, and believe it were unfairly given. But suffered a lot from my sisters afterwards and for many years just the mention of our names, mentioned together, made me boiling mad. That and the fact that we were the very same age brought on a correspondence in later years that enabled her to "snare" me."*

Sharing the same birth date of February 6, 1888, Perley would refer to Helen in his letters as his *"twin sister."* Their contact, however, was limited to short notes between distant acquaintances, definitely not what one would consider love letters. It doesn't appear that Perley ever gave much forethought to marrying Helen. Even a letter written between them just two weeks before their wedding was formal and impersonal, giving no indication of their plans to wed!

Helen, however, had ideas of her own and made it quite plain in her letters, to anyone less naïve than Perley, that she was in the market for a husband. When Perley was thinking of buying his farm, she wrote: *"Would you live there alone? Don't you ever get lonesome?"* She continued even more pointedly, *"Don't know but what this place* [the house her family was renting] *will be sold in the spring. I suppose I shall have to sell my cattle (I own 7 head). I don't want to. I had rather be on a farm."* As further reinforcement she wrote, *"I think 'twins' ought to know each other better than we do, don't you?"* And just in case he missed all of her other hints, she offered, *"Am making me a white dress."*

Perley

Helen's parents had separated when she was a teenager. Her mother had moved out leaving the children in the custody of their father. Helen had no choice but to take over the care of her family. Always a hard worker, in addition to doing household chores and looking after the livestock, Helen also held jobs in town. Though she seemed to accept her role as family caretaker without complaint, at age twenty-two Helen wanted a home of her own. And it finally struck Perley that she might be the "perfect" wife he needed to help care for his farm and bear his future children.

Seeing each other very little during the intervening years, Perley was unaware that Helen had grown into a tall, slim and quite attractive young woman. When they finally met again he was immediately captivated. Helen had a serious and quiet demeanor that appealed to Perley. He found her to be very "feminine." He had always been attracted to brunettes and Helen had long, soft waving brown hair that she often wore up in a loose bun.

Helen Whitney seemed the answer to his dreams. Unable to believe his good luck that such an appealing woman was willing and actually anxious to marry him and move to his isolated farm, Perley saw no reason to postpone matters. On July 15, 1911, Helen and Perley were married in a small ceremony at Perley's home, much to the surprise and delight of his family. Two weeks later a reception was held with Perley's family and friends. The East Sullivan band played and cake, cookies and lemonade were served.

Helen moved into Perley's home and set about giving it a woman's touch. Being an experienced seamstress (*"once I intended to be a dressmaker"*), Helen sewed curtains for the windows, adding color and comfort to each room. She mended Perley's clothes, giving them a fine stitching rather than the "make-do" repair job he was forced to perform before his marriage. His home soon took on a charming aura, with hand stitched pillows and quilted wall hangings, reminiscent of his life when he lived with his mother and four sisters. Perley was glad to have a female presence once again. He was proud of his new wife, a woman with an agreeable personality who tried hard to please him.

In turn, Helen enjoyed taking care of her own home. Left in charge of the household, she dedicated herself to making it as pleasant and comfortable as possible. Perley fully supported her by buying new material for her sewing projects. Both of them enjoyed showing off the improvements to their home whenever neighbors and family came to call.

As a young girl Helen had not been close to her own mother. To be warmly received by Elsie Jane made her feel special. Helen especially enjoyed having sisters; for the first time in her life she had the female companionship that had been missing. And it felt good to be welcomed into the neighborhood and treated with respect as Perley's new wife.

Helen did, however, have a strong will. Spending the last few years at home caretaking her father and brothers had kept that independent streak well hidden. Though Helen ostensibly was mild-mannered, content to let her husband make the decisions during her early marriage, that strong will would gradually surface. Some of her views of a woman's place in the marriage were, perhaps, a little more modern than Elsie Jane's had been. As a result, Helen was not quite as willing to submit to her husband's absolute authority. This and other circumstances would lead to marital disharmony in later years.

But for now, each of them exhibited their best behavior. In many ways still strangers, they settled into a comfortable routine. Both worked from morning till night to improve the farm, planning a prosperous future for themselves and for the children they hoped they'd have.

Perley

After a hard day working around their farm, Perley looked forward to sitting down at the kitchen table to a good, home cooked meal. Helen proved to be an excellent cook, preparing tasty dishes from the vegetables they grew and game Perley hunted on their land. Finishing with his favorite desserts, pies baked with Helen's hand-picked berries and apples, Perley was content, as is conveyed by this stanza of one of his poems.

> *"I need you to cook and wash and mend,*
> *But more than that I want you should care;*
> *Just to have you beside me and encouragement lend,*
> *Will mean that what I with you gain, with you*
> *I would share."*

Perley anxiously anticipated their private moments at bedtime together and having Helen's loving arms around him as he slept. In the early days of their married life they loved to cuddle under the quilts and whisper of the future they would share. Talk would turn to children as they discussed how many they hoped to have and the names that appealed to both of them. Their future looked hopeful as newlyweds.

During those late night discussions, however, Helen never mentioned the dark memories that were weighing so heavily on her. She was trying hard to be the perfect wife she knew Perley wanted and expected. But the secrets of her past were gnawing at her. How she must have dreaded the day when those secrets would come spilling out.

Perley as a young man of twenty-one

Perley's house in Sullivan, NH
"Old Hastings House" around 1909

Helen Eva (Whitney) and Perley Swett
Taken around 1911

Chapter Five
Secrets of the Past

Helen's desire to marry Perley on short notice may have had more to do with her need to get away from her family home than with her attraction to him. Helen's childhood had been neither happy nor secure. Her father, Edgar Rand Whitney, was the black sheep of an otherwise hardworking and prosperous family. Unlike his father and brother who accumulated a sizable amount of property, Edgar was never able to hold onto a job or a place to live. Constantly moving his family from one rented house to another, Helen never had a place she could call home.

Growing up in a very troubled household, Helen was surrounded by constant fighting between her mother and father. Though there is no record of physical abuse, Helen witnessed firsthand the mental suffering her mother was forced to put up with. Unlike Perley's eventual acceptance of his parent's life together as being an appropriate role model for a marriage, Helen vowed that she would never tolerate the same treatment that her mother had endured.

Whether Perley actually proposed to Helen or they simply made a mutual decision in the heat of the moment, once talk turned to marriage Helen was anxious to move quickly. She did not tell her father of their plans until after the wedding took place. Perley did not question her motives, interpreting her urgency as a compliment. He also came to suspect that Mr. Whitney might be upset at the thought of losing his housekeeper and, given his drinking habit, would try to make trouble for them. (Perley remembered the problems with his own father when he was drinking and didn't want to deal with Edgar under those circumstances.) Helen's mother had already written to Perley to warn him about Edgar. *"He is probably all out of money and will want some to buy liquor with. Don't let Helen let him have any."*

Less than two weeks after their wedding, when Perley was away from home working at a neighbor's, Helen's father made his first of several upsetting visits. It was mid-morning and Helen had just started heating a pot of water to wash clothes. When she heard the front door open she assumed Perley had forgotten something and eagerly went to greet him. Instead, Helen found herself face to face with her father. Fighting the urge to flee, she bravely faced him. Even at that early hour, Edgar had been drinking, was quite angry and demanded that Helen return home with him. Though fearful of disobeying her father, Helen refused. She was a married woman now and an adult in the eyes of the law. Edgar, however, knew how to control her. He had successfully intimidated Helen for most of her life and had no intention of stopping now.

What Perley would not find out until later was that during those first few months of their marriage, Edgar was blackmailing Helen, insisting she continue to *"be a wife to him as well as to Perley."* If Helen did not comply, Edgar threatened to tell Perley about their previous relationship. This was what Helen feared most. She hadn't told Perley that she was the victim of incest. It was a horrible life from which she had escaped and Helen feared that if she had told Perley the truth before the wedding he might not want her for his wife. And that fear would prove to be well founded.

Perley

It had started when Helen was just thirteen. By the time she turned fifteen her mother, Emma, discovered what was happening and filed charges against Edgar for child abuse. The case never reached the court; it was said that Edgar paid Emma $700, all the money he had, to drop the charges. Whether Emma agreed to this out of fear, greed or belief that Edgar would change his ways is hard to fathom. Within a few years Emma and her husband split up. Though it must have tormented her to do so, Emma felt she had no choice but to leave Helen and her two youngest brothers in the custody of their father. Left destitute with few ways to support herself, Emma was forced to live with any family member who would have her.

Helen felt completely abandoned. Now there was no one she could turn to for protection. Many people in town knew or suspected what was happening but there were no social services to intervene. Nor did any family member want to get involved. A young man Helen had a crush on would *"not give her notice because of what was said about her in town."* If Helen was to escape her situation, it would be up to her to do so. When the opportunity to marry Perley presented itself, it was the Godsend she prayed for and Helen was determined not to let this chance slip through her fingers.

Out of fear of Edgar's threat to expose her "deception," Helen continued her relationship with her father on three more occasions after her wedding before she finally refused his intimidation. This was in November and Helen realized she was pregnant. She resolved to make a stand against her father. Perhaps, she reasoned, Perley loved her enough by now to accept her past and forgive her for not telling him. (In later years, neither Perley nor Helen questioned the paternity of this first child. It seems odd that they wouldn't but whatever their reasons were, they felt assured that the child was, indeed, Perley's.)

On December 12, 1911, just five months after Perley and Helen were married, Helen's father returned again to her new home to confront Helen once more about coming back *"to keep house for him."* A newspaper account described what happened next. Edgar, while out deer hunting, had been drinking heavily. When he arrived at Helen's doorstep, wielding his rifle, she refused to let him in. At this time Edgar *"began acting queerly"* and threatened to kill himself. Scared, Helen ran out the back door to get away from him and find help. She had only gone a short distance when she heard a gun shot. Running back, she found her father sprawled on her front step, his face covered in blood and gore. Edgar had propped his rifle on his boot, held it under his chin and shot himself. Because of the way his head was tilted back due to the length of the rifle *"the bullet took an upward course through the chin and came out above the nose. Part of his tongue was grazed, the jaw bones broken, the palate torn away and the nasal bone fractured, leaving a huge gap where the nose should be."*

Helen was able to summon Perley from the field and he ran to the neighbor's to call for a doctor who, upon arriving, transported Edgar immediately to the hospital. While he was on the operating table Edgar ceased breathing and physicians performed an emergency tracheotomy.

Amazingly, Edgar Whitney survived his suicide attempt. The doctors patched him up and sewed his nose back together. In time, he moved back to his home and hired a young housekeeper. The poor girl must have been totally desperate. Though Edgar was fifty-two at the time and the housekeeper was only twenty-one, she consented to marry him and ultimately bore him another daughter.

With her father finally out of the picture, Perley and Helen should have had better prospects to settle into a long and happy marriage. Their first child was on the way, they had a nice home and their future was full of promise. But by now, Helen had confessed her secrets to Perley and, as she feared, Perley was not in a forgiving mood.

Once Perley discovered the truth about Helen's years of forced incest with her father he was shocked and hurt by her deception and feared that others would come to know, and judge him by, her background. He said *"for no more could he live with her, if made public was her past."* In one of his poems Perley says to Helen *"I didn't want you to tell your shame to the world."* Was he trying to protect her reputation or his own pride?

It was tragic that Perley could not understand Helen's suffering and realize that its cause was beyond her control. But it was a different time one hundred years ago and the victim of incest was often stigmatized, made to feel guilty for her own abuse. Unfortunately, Perley's behavior dealt more with his fears about what his neighbors might think, or being seen as a cuckold, than with Helen's feelings.

A product of his own upbringing, with parental relationships that left him with strong narcissistic leanings, Perley could only see Helen's relationship with her father, having taken place after their wedding, as evidence of disloyalty to him. In Perley's mind Helen was part of a willing conspiracy...and that conspiracy had violated *not Helen* but, simply, the marriage trust. Likely, Perley's worst fear was that Helen did not and never had loved him and had only used him to escape her father. His pride did not allow him to express this fear so, instead, he chose to place the blame on Helen and, to mask his own pain, remained militantly unforgiving.

Perley's best and worst trait was pride. To his credit, throughout his life he always tried to be fair and honest and do what he felt was morally right. He considered himself a paragon of virtue. He never lied, cheated or stole from anyone. His most prized possession was his "good name."

When Perley learned that the wife who vowed to love, honor and cherish him had tarnished his good reputation and, in his opinion, played him for a fool, he was devastated. In a rage, he swore he would divorce Helen.

*"When I found out you had deceived me and was
untrue the first month you were my bride,
I should have divorced you then but for your tears
and threats to be a suicide."*

Helen begged him to stay, threatening to kill herself if he left her. Pregnant with their first son, Helen was terrified of being deserted by her husband. Where would she go? Remembering her mother's humiliating plight of being passed from one relative to another, she was fearful of finding herself in the same situation. In desperation she promised Perley that she would never again be "unfaithful" or lie to him and would always be a good and loving wife.

Perley had always envisioned leading an idealized life with a loving wife and loving children working side by side with him on a prosperous farm. He did not want the scandal a divorce would bring nor could he forgive and forget what had been done to his dream by "a wife such as that."

Finally, after much pleading on Helen's part, Perley grudgingly agreed to stay in their marriage, though he would expect Helen to constantly prove her love and gratitude as her penance. At first she was thankful for Perley's concession but when confronted by his continuing disapproval and demands, Helen found renewed strength over time. She would finally stop blaming herself for what had happened. And in the years ahead, Perley found it increasingly difficult to live with Helen's growing independence.

Their first son, Harvey, was born the following year in June, 1912. Elsie Jane wrote with pride, *"Perley built a crib*

Perley

for him with castors on it." Two more sons, Richard and Maurice, quickly followed. Through the next twenty years Perley and Helen labored side by side to establish a prosperous and sometimes even a happy home for their children. Unfortunately, both Perley and Helen had more than their share of stubborn pride. Neither was actually willing to forgive and forget the pain they felt had been inflicted by the other. Anger and resentment can often stay deeply buried while two people are busy raising a family. At some point, though, it always finds its way back to the surface.

* * *

Late one night during the winter of 1912, an unexpected knock sounded at the door. Perley opened it to find one of his neighbors leaning out of breath against the door frame. *"There's been an accident on the pond. We need help to search. Bring a lantern, quick!"* Perley grabbed his coat and lantern and ran with the man through the woods on the path to Bolster Pond.

"What happened?" Perley asked.

"The Fifields and some others were skating on the pond," the neighbor called out breathlessly, *"Frank Fifield was pushing everyone around on the ice in his skating chair. There was thin ice and open water around the back of the pond. Frank stayed away from that side all night. Then it was the strangest thing."* The neighbor stopped running long enough to catch his breath and look Perley in the face, *"At the end of the night when everyone else was done, he gives his wife, Lottie, a ride and seemed to head straight for the back side of the pond. No one heard nothin but when they didn't come back the others hollered for them. They ain't been seen since."*

Perley couldn't believe what he was hearing. Frank and Lottie Fifield had been his good friends and neighbors for years. When one of Perley's steers had gotten his nose filled with porcupine quills the Fifields had helped remove them. He'd spent many a relaxing evening playing checkers with Frank and Lottie had cut his hair for his wedding. Perley had watched their two young daughters grow since they were born. This couldn't be happening.

As they reached the pond other neighbors had already arrived and, with lanterns and long sticks, were searching the water under the ice. The Fifield's two young daughters had been taken home to be with their grandfather who lived with them. As the old man saw the girls being brought home without their parents he sensed what must have happened. *"It's Frank and Lottie isn't it?"* his voice cracked.

The local newspaper described the incident as follows: *"The ice was too thin to admit much searching on foot and a boat was put into use. The chair and Mrs. Fifield's cloak were found and later, between 11:30 and 12 o'clock her body was taken from the water. The search kept up and Mr. Fifield's body was discovered near the same spot about 9:30 this morning."* It went on to say, *"The skating expedition was a most foolish procedure, for it is said an ax dropped on the ice went through."* The newspaper account also reported that Frank Fifield had gone down to the pond earlier in the evening before the skating party to see *"if skating was possible."* Surely he must have had some idea where the ice was the weakest...

The deaths of Mr. and Mrs. Fifield were always deemed suspicious though no one ever really knew what had happened. Helen wrote in her diary that Lottie Fifield weighed 350 pounds. Why her husband would be pushing her around on ice of questionable thickness does seem a little hard to comprehend. In a letter to Elsie Jane, another neighbor put into words what most people were thinking at the time: "*It was an awful accident the drowning of the Fifields and such a careless way! It would almost seem suicide and murder!*" Perhaps Perley and Helen were not the only ones having trouble in their marriage.

Edgar Rand Whitney after he shot himself
Born January 19, 1861 - Died June 23, 1938

Chapter Six
A Visitor

Most days Perley and Helen were exhausted by day's end. It was easier for them to ignore dealing with their marital problems than trying to fix them. And there would be more chores the next day to distract them from working toward a solution. So the days, and their uneasy collaboration, marched on. Then, on April 24, 1918, during the seventh year of their life together, Helen presented Perley with a gift that meant more to him than anything she had done or would ever do again. For a while at least he would be willing to "forgive her" for her perceived transgressions. On that day Helen gave birth to beautiful twin girls.

Perley was ecstatic. Perhaps this was the magic potion that would heal the marriage - a gift not simply from a repentant wife but from a benevolent Almighty, both repaying Perley for the pain he'd been put through.

"When girls came and twins, life seemed going fine,
 To make up for sorrow, to me they were sent;
I gave wife the boys but called the girls mine,
 Stored up love had a chance now to be spent."

These four lines of poetry capture the way Perley viewed his marriage at the time. Not only had his marriage partner let him down, his sons had been a disappointment to him also.

A Visitor

Perley was authoritarian, demanding perfection (as he saw it) from his wife and young sons, aged three to six. While his demeanor may have commanded obedience, it apparently did not engender the degree of affection he sought. There was a coolness between him and his wife. And in their youthful exuberance, his young sons had already learned to be cautious about how they approached him. Having had a distant relationship with his own father, it is likely that Perley may not have been able to form a warm and loving relationship with his own sons. Now, perhaps the "miracle" of twin daughters would bring Perley not simply respect but the love and affection he desperately needed. In turn, his own "stored up love" could be spent on something worthy.

Perley began at once to make a special place for them. *"When the twins came,"* Elsie Jane wrote proudly to a friend, *"the old crib wouldn't do so Perley made another nice one big enough for two and put casters on that one."*

At this pivotal point in their lives, Helen used Perley's happiness to her advantage, getting him to agree to her request that he *"show his love and appreciation for her"* by destroying the letter her father, Edgar, had sent her years earlier in which he admitted their incestuous relationship. Unfortunately, this newfound marital peace and harmony was not to last and Perley would regret having taken this action some years later when he needed proof of his wife's "affair."

* * *

During the summer of 1918, while Perley was still utterly captivated with his baby daughters, a most unlikely visitor entered his remote neck of the woods. A worldly and wealthy woman by the name of Florence Brooks happened upon Perley's isolated corner of the world and was so enthralled with its pristine beauty and solitude, she decided to make it her new home. In ways she could never imagine, this decision would cause her life to become deeply entwined with that of Perley's family. For she would choose to build a lavish estate here and Perley and his family would be her closest neighbors in the wilderness.

Why Florence chose to build there was fodder for town gossip for several years. She was a woman who was used to a life of luxury in New York City. Her new neighbors, mostly poor farmers eking out a living from their lands, could not understand why anyone would trade a life of ease and pampering for the hardships of living in a near wilderness, deep in the woods of their small New Hampshire town.

Florence Brooks, however, had no intention of giving up her opulent lifestyle. Her plans were extravagant and included creating a grand estate in unspoiled wilderness, one with extensive flower gardens, Italian statuary, a man-made lake and access roads laid out through the thick woods. For this was an era when the wealthy built country "cottages" in the Adirondacks and elsewhere, lavish retreats from the city where friends in society could experience "nature" in a most comfortable manner.

Gossip was flowing fast and furious about this new arrival. Perley and his family, along with the rest of the town, watched with great curiosity as their new neighbor prepared to build what she called her *"cabin in the woods."* (This first small cottage would be a place she would live in until her main lodge could be built.)

Florence Cornelia Ellwanger came into the world on Christmas Day, 1875, in Rochester, New York. She was born into a family whose prosperity went back several generations. The family fortune began with her grandfather, George Ellwanger, who had been born in Wurttemburg, Germany. His youth was spent with his father and brothers in the family's vineyards. He later served as an apprentice in a leading nursery in Stuttgart before migrating to America. George liked the area of Rochester, New York, and took a job at Reynolds & Bateman Nursery. In 1840 he linked up with Patrick Barry and, together, formed the Ellwanger & Barry Nursery which later became the Mount Hope Nurseries of Rochester, New York. It flourished to the point of becoming one of the largest establishments of its kind at the turn of the century.

In 1846 George Ellwanger married Cornelia Brooks. Their first son, George Herman Ellwanger was born July 10, 1848. George Herman also became a successful businessman and author as well. Carrying on the family's horticulture tradition, he wrote several books on gardening and amassed the largest collection of tea roses in America. For many years he was the owner and editor of the Rochester Post Express. In his obituary it was written of him, *"Few men ever had a more intense consciousness of the loveliness of the world we live in."*

The Ellwanger line continued after George Herman married Harriet Stillson and she gave birth to their three daughters, Florence Cornelia, Laura Brooks, and Julia Stillson.

Florence Cornelia Ellwanger lived a privileged life growing up, that of a young debutante. She attended fine private schools, both in this country and abroad. As a young woman, she traveled extensively in Europe and enjoyed social interaction with the rich and famous of her day.

Florence's father and grandfather were friends and neighbors of George Eastman. Although financially successful in their own right, the Ellwangers invested heavily in his new startup company, Eastman Kodak. In time, Florence would inherit a sizable share of her family's fortune, enabling her to maintain her life of privilege and become involved in a number of philanthropic endeavors.

As a young woman, who had led a pampered life, Florence may have had a rebellious streak. She married Albert W. Lilienthal, her first husband, apparently without parental blessing. That marriage lasted less than five years. As she wrote to a friend, *"my husband left me alone without support with Albert Jr. yet unborn. My family were angry with me when I married him."* It is possible that her family may have disowned her for a time as she spoke years later of an elderly aunt who was the only one to help her through this difficult period in her life.

Florence had a strong will. Neither tall nor particularly slim, she had an ample figure and was what one might call a "handsome" woman. Said variously to be "a man's woman" and to have a "loud personality," she was willing to pay for what she wanted but would expect full value in return.

In later life Florence would be equally comfortable dripping in furs and diamonds or decked out in hunting clothes, seemingly ready to hunt wild game. Whether she was a difficult person to live with or chose her life partners poorly, we do not know. But after her marriage to Albert Lilienthal ended, two more brief marriages would follow, each ending in divorce.

During the next few years, Florence continued to be very active in both charities and the arts. During World War I, while her seventeen year old son served as a bomber, she worked with both the Red Cross and the lesser known Blue Cross. Florence was especially interested in the work of the latter organization. The Blue Cross cared for horses and dogs trained to work at the front in the war.

Hundreds of soldiers blinded in the war also benefited from the generosity of Florence Brooks, as she came to be known when she took her mother's maiden name. Mrs. Brooks donated thousands of dollars to numerous charities in her lifetime and shared not only her fortune but also her time and energy.

Before and after the war, Florence traveled extensively throughout Europe. Having studied at the Conservatory of Music and Art at Stuttgart, Germany, she was a well-educated woman living a luxurious life. At one point she had several different addresses in New York City, including a posh residence at 55 Park Avenue.

One must ask, therefore, why this socialite - seemingly content and in her forties - headed deep into the woods of southwestern New Hampshire to seek *"peace and quiet out of the city's turmoil and unrest."* Whatever her reasons, Florence fell in love with a *"2 acre setting on the edge of a beautiful mill pond, completely surrounded by mountains, where over a hundred years previous a most profitable old mill operated."*

It was during the ensuing year that Florence met the man who would become her fourth husband, Arthur Mills Aten. A miner by trade, it was said that she promised to marry him if he would build her a log cabin on her new property. Evidently Mr. Aten was agreeable as they were married shortly thereafter on September 28, 1919. Immediately a most unusual partnership began.

While Florence continued to travel between her homes in New York and Europe where she stayed with friends, Arthur set to work making Florence's "cabin in the woods" a reality. Legend has it that he lived in a tent on the property through that first winter while building their home, and came to rely on his closest neighbors for help and companionship. It was only natural that Arthur would enjoy an occasional home cooked meal and the conversation he would find with Perley's family. Perhaps it was simply due to Florence's extended absences from Arthur's side or his Spartan existence living alone in a tent, but Perley began to think that Arthur was becoming too constant a presence at his table.

In March, Helen became pregnant once again, the circumstances of which Perley came to question in the years to come. This child and last son, Warren Daniel, was born December 16, 1920. All of Helen's children had been born at home and the births had gone fairly smoothly. But Helen was now thirty-two and had already borne five children. This birth, her sixth, was a very difficult one for Helen. As Perley later wrote she *"came very near to dying by losing so much blood."* The doctor had to be called to apply packing to stop the bleeding. Perley, ever miserly, sent a letter of complaint to the doctor afterwards about his bill, arguing that the doctor needn't have made a second trip to treat his wife that same day. *"Mrs. Swett or a neighbor lady could have changed the packing."* Perley wrote, adding, *"If you had charged me for only one visit, I would have felt that was a just and reasonable bill and that you were honest and trying to use me right."* Clearly the gulf that existed between Perley and Helen at that point had hardened. His concern for his wife's welfare did not rise above his belief that money should only be spent on what he deemed absolute necessities.

In the end, to placate Perley, the doctor agreed to lower the bill but only after stating that due to Perley's strong wording in his letter (*"the extravagant way you have expressed yourself"*) that *"whenever you are again in need of a doctor, kindly send for Dr. Hildreth or Taft."*

Helen vowed that this would be her last child. Her health was not good and she did not dare risk having more children. Perley, however, remained unconcerned. He viewed children as assets, much the same as land. Both, when acquired, were signs of success. Helen, at this point in her life, felt quite the opposite. She wrote in secret to Margaret Sanger of New York City.

Margaret Sanger was one of the first leaders of the Birth Control movement. She was born in 1879 as Margaret Louise Higgins and had, as the oldest child, watched her mother struggle through eighteen pregnancies producing eleven live births before she, herself, died of tuberculosis at the age of fifty.

Margaret was deeply concerned about the state of ignorance in which her mother and many women of low socioeconomic status found themselves. Women of wealth had access to information about limiting their family size. But poor, working-class women accepted a servitude of yearly pregnancies, miscarriages and botched abortions. Shocked by the inability of most women to obtain accurate and effective birth control Margaret became a crusader, challenging the 1873 federal Comstock Law which banned the distribution of contraceptive information. She also published a radical feminist magazine titled, "The Woman Rebel."

Margaret argued for limiting the size of families. She wanted to help working class women to avoid the economic pitfalls and health problems of unwanted pregnancies. In 1912, she wrote a column on sex education for the New York Call entitled 'What every girl should know'. Censors attempted to suppress her column on venereal disease, deeming it obscene.

Several issues of the magazine were banned and Sanger was indicted for violating postal obscenity laws. Before fleeing the country for a short time to avoid imprisonment, she instructed friends to release to the public 100,000 copies of "Family Limitation," a 16 page pamphlet which provided detailed instructions on the uses of birth control.

A copy of this pamphlet is undoubtedly what Helen was seeking when she wrote to Sanger in 1921. At the same time Perley ignored her pleas not to have more children. What Helen may have learned from Margaret Sanger or if she put that knowledge into practice is not known. But she did not become pregnant again - until almost ten years later!

Perley and Helen's twin girls
Dora and Dorothy Swett - Born April 24, 1918

Florence Brooks Aten
Born December 25, 1875

L-R: Richard Swett, Helen holding twins, Harvey Swett, Emma Harvey Whitney, Maurice Swett

Chapter Seven
Lives Intertwined

For better or worse, Elsie Jane and Daniel, Perley and Helen, and Florence and Arthur Aten were becoming more and more involved in each other's daily lives. And 1922 proved to be an eventful year for this triangle of neighbors.

Arthur Aten was putting the finishing touches on Florence's cabin, called "Shinbone Shack." It was so named because the shinbones of a moose were found during excavation and cemented into the hearth of the stone fireplace. They remained there for more than half a century. And although Florence loved her little *cottage in the woods,* her dream was still to build an elegant Adirondack-type lodge where she would spend her remaining years in style and comfort. Had she had more modest ambitions for her estate at Wood's Mill she might have survived the hard times that lay ahead. But she had much loftier plans in mind.

Arthur continued to spend much of his time alone in Stoddard, clearing and reshaping the land as Florence traveled between the cabin in Stoddard and her apartment and charity work in New York City. It seems likely their union was more a marriage of convenience than a love match, at least to Florence.

While Florence was busy planning her dream estate, all was not going well in Perley's house. He and Helen had begun bickering again and, to add to their stress, tragedy was about to strike.

There was no plumbing in Perley and Helen's house at the time. Water ran downhill from a spring through pipes and into a large wooden barrel stored in a back shed. The family scooped out water as they needed it. One day while Helen was outside hanging laundry, their infant son, Warren Daniel, wandered alone into the back room and climbed onto a crate which was beside the water barrel. At only eighteen-months old and having no sense of fear, he leaned too far over the edge and fell into the barrel head first. Unable to pull himself back out, he drowned. It was a tragic accident and Helen, as any mother would, blamed herself for not watching him more closely. Perley did nothing to ease that guilt. In fact, Perley had already entertained dark thoughts about whether Warren Daniel was, in fact, his own child. He didn't look like any of their other children. And Perley thought he had noticed some furtive looks exchanged between Helen and Arthur Aten from time to time.

Shortly before Warren Daniel died, Arthur Aten mysteriously left Wood's Mill, sent packing by his wife with $3,000 and a one way ticket to Hawaii. Many years later in a letter dated March 2, 1947, to his brother-in-law, Charles Partridge, Perley confided in him, *"I do not know definitely whether I am right or wrong, but I have always suspected the boy that died was not mine and because he was going to look too much like his father was the cause of his death. The man was several thousand miles away before I happened to find out what had been going on. She* [Helen] *admitted then to her improper relations with him but didn't admit she began until after this baby had been born."*

This disturbing letter raises many questions. Did Perley honestly believe Helen capable of murdering her own child? Did Helen really have an affair with Arthur Aten or was she simply trying to hurt Perley by falsely confessing to one? Why did Arthur Aten leave so suddenly for Hawaii? And how much of all this conjecture was due to Perley's fears, the tormented thoughts of a husband deeply wounded once again by his wife's unfaithfulness?

We'll never know. But during the next year Perley purchased the necessary supplies and installed plumbing in his house. Arthur Aten did write one last letter, postmarked from Hawaii, to Perley's father, Daniel. In it he asked Daniel to look after and *"see that Mrs. Aten is safe. You know how much I love her. Help her every way you can."* By the time the letter arrived, however, in September of 1922, Perley's father had already quietly passed away at the age of eighty-three.

With his father gone, Perley found himself caring for his mother and her property as well as his own. At the same time, Florence Aten again found herself without a husband and needed help to make her grand plans a reality. She had a growing list of tasks she needed to accomplish and the money to have them done. But she needed manpower. If she ever shared Perley's suspicions about her husband and Helen, she was too proud to ever let them show. Whatever her thoughts were, she did not seem to harbor any resentment toward the Swett family. In fact, she turned to them more and more for help in the years to come.

Always one to recognize a good business arrangement, Perley joined forces with his new neighbor and made himself invaluable as her groundskeeper, watchman and all around handyman. He did whatever odd jobs she asked of him and soon became indispensable not only as an employee she could trust but also as a friend. *"If everyone was as fair as you have been this would be a better world"* Florence often told him. Because Florence traveled so extensively while work proceeded on her property, Perley became her eyes and ears, inspecting and supervising work on her estate on his daily rounds.

Perley's new job gave his family a steady income and a chance for the first time in their lives for a little prosperity. One neighbor remembered visiting the twins to play when she was a young girl. She recalled that they *"always had nicer dolls because Perley worked for a rich woman."* Mrs. Aten would often bring dolls and toys back from her world travels as gifts for Perley's children.

Florence also began buying up parcels of land adjoining her property, paying outrageous prices from those who knew how anxious she was to increase her holdings. Over the next several years she purchased a total of 1200 acres from neighboring landowners who were more than willing to sell their unproductive forest land at top dollar. It seems likely that Perley watched Florence's land acquisitions closely, learning from her mistakes. Perley was always on the lookout to further his own land purchases should investment opportunities present themselves.

To begin development of Florence's new estate, architects, contractors and laborers needed to be hired. An expensive, two mile long road was built into her valley with gravel brought in from several miles away. In Florence's excitement to begin work on her new home, she made a careless mistake. A section of her new road was laid out through a quarter mile of land that did not belong to her. Knowing the area, Perley recognized this, but instead of going to Florence and pointing out her mistake he quietly purchased the twenty-five acre lot through which the road passed and held on to it. *"She did not realize she was not the owner of this parcel,"* Perley wrote to a friend some years later, *"that she had spent about $20,000.00 on building a road, bridges, and a twenty-inch water main and cable buried to another foundation for a second power house a few hundred feet lower down on* *brook.*" Whether Perley was doing this to protect Florence, or turn her mistake to his own advantage, is hard to say. He held onto this investment parcel for many years until the right opportunity to dispose of it came along.

The most ambitious aspect of Florence's estate building project was to be her mansion. To achieve this end, Florence hired Augustus D. Shepard, a well-known New York architect specializing in Adirondack style "cottages." Shepard's style and the country homes he designed were popular with wealthy New Yorkers looking to escape the city. No longer content with the primitive and rustic cabins of the 1880s, Augustus Shepard created summer homes in the woods. They were built with the best materials money could buy and they provided every modern convenience available at the time.

Shepard felt it was necessary to consider the view when planning the placement of various windows in the main living rooms. He wrote, "*The reflection of the woods and mountains in the still waters of the lake makes a picture dear to the heart of the camp owner.*" With this in mind, Mr. Shepard designed a lodge for Florence with an enormous two story picture window, facing her own private lake and wooded mountainside.

To take better advantage of the waterside setting outside her door, Florence had the pond enlarged, lining much of it with boulders and rebuilt the dam. This she ornamented with old granite mill wheels. To provide electricity, she built a new stone power house complete with an eight foot tall water wheel at the lower end of the pond below the dam. It was driven by a large underground pipe which, when a valve was opened, allowed water to be diverted from the pond to a wooden sluice atop the water wheel. The water wheel, in turn, drove a generator inside the powerhouse. An underground cable ran from the power house to a large electrical panel with huge copper circuit breakers in the basement of the new house...an arrangement that looked like (as the present owner described it) *"something out of a Frankenstein movie."* In his book, *Camps In The Woods*, the architect Augustus Shepard includes drawings and pictures of Florence Brooks-Aten's lodge under construction. In it he describes this powerhouse and wheel as adding a "picturesque note to the property."

A separate winter power house was begun but never completed. Don Healy, the present owner of Florence's estate, described it as a *"concrete bunker about 100 yards downstream of the water wheel. It was designed to house an underwater turbine of some sort that would be able to run with water flowing under the ice at times when the water wheel would have frozen up. A separate pipe with a shut-off valve was installed to direct water to this turbine."*

A neighbor and local historian, Pheroba Wilson, visited with Florence when her lodge was being built. As she later described in the Stoddard Town History, *"After her workmen left for the night [Florence] would sit alone in the lodge, soon to be finished, and look up at the high vaulted ceiling and the galleries along the walls. Then, her back to the great fieldstone fireplace, she would look out through the scaffolding of what was to be an enormous picture window to the dark wooded hill to the south. Here, standing high above the spruce cover, stood two giant old-growth trees; her Indian Chieftain and his princess, the last to catch the rays of the setting sun."*

Next, Florence put in a garden. But it would not be just any garden. She had also inherited her family's love of horticulture. To put that love to work she had stonemasons build a Japanese garden across the lake from her lodge, one with high sculptured stonewalls that would protect the exotic plants she chose from woodland creatures. Her estate was further accented with Italian statuary. Florence's utopia deep in the Stoddard Woods was becoming a reality...a most expensive reality.

For all of her grand ideas, and coming from a markedly different background, Florence Brooks-Aten seemed to develop and enjoy warm relationships with her country neighbors. They treated her with kindness and made her feel welcome in their homes. Florence became close friends with Elsie Jane, whom she called "Mother Swett." Never one to receive without giving in return, Mrs. Aten brought them watermelons from her garden, ice cream that she made herself and bananas she brought back from her trips to New York City. She attended Thanksgiving Dinner at Elsie Jane's house, contributing a plump store-bought turkey. And at Christmas Florence gave toys to Perley's children. She especially liked to spoil the twins.

Florence enjoyed children and always had candy ready to pass out to children of friends and of the men who worked for her. One recipient of Florence's generosity would recall years later, *"Mrs. Aten never seemed like a real person, more of a movie star."*

An unusual symbiosis had developed between Mrs. Brooks-Aten and Perley. A most unlikely duo given their backgrounds, talents and employer-employee relationship, each benefited from working closely together. What they shared in common was their deep love of the land. Why they felt that way could not have been more different, however. Florence acquired land to enable her to build her sanctuary, a place of quiet beauty she could shape according to her own wishes...a unique reflection of who she was. To Perley, land had quite another value. Land could be worked for the goods it might produce. Land could also be bought and sold for a profit. Land would be his way to acquire wealth and prestige. And if Perley could become one of Stoddard's largest landowners, he believed that would earn him the respect and admiration of his peers. By working together on their properties, Perley and Florence advanced their separate agendas, Perley by saving and Florence by spending.

* * *

During their years of marital turmoil, Perley and Helen's children were growing up fast. They were involved in the 4-H club as were many farm youngsters from the country towns. This also gave them a chance to escape from the tense atmosphere at home. They participated in such programs as poultry judging and forestry projects which gave children the opportunity to win free trips to camp. One of their projects involved transplanting 6,975 white pine seedlings. As members of the county canning team, the now almost teenage twin girls "put up" 148-quarts of vegetables, 63-quarts of fruits, 32-quarts of pickles and 8-quarts of jelly one summer, winning them second place in a contest.

Being familiar with hard work at home on the farm, there was very little that the children couldn't accomplish. While Perley did not lavish on his sons a great deal of warmth and affection, he was a good teacher, passing on to them the skills and practical knowledge they would need to become self sufficient later in life. The children were old enough now to help regularly with the chores and work with their father to cut pine off the land for extra income. In a journal kept by Perley's oldest son, Harvey, in 1926 when he was fourteen years old, he wrote daily of the work he did on the farm. Many of these chores were carried out no differently than when Elsie Jane or Perley were young themselves. In a stunningly similar writing style this third generation Swett recorded his own farm chores.

> *"Went down to help plow in field north of Mrs. Aten's road. Had test in school*
>
> *Helped level off sods that Papa drew for filling at Mrs. Aten's*
>
> *Went over to Gramma Swett's and worked in garden*
>
> *Worked in garden setting out plants, helped Papa take down load of hay*
>
> *Picked blueberries, turned oats back of barn, helped hay, mowed and raked*
>
> *Worked at Mrs. Aten's, got sticks and lily pads out of pond*
>
> *Went up to Gramma Swett's and picked some pears up to the Whittier place, and some gooseberries without thorns at the other place, went down to Aten's and helped move some stones."*

In addition to their tasks around the house, Helen expected her children to attend school. She felt an education was important, especially for her sons. In the future this would be another source of disagreement between her and Perley.

The children were also expected to help "Grammy Swett" care for her nearby homestead now that she was alone. All of Elsie Jane's children were married by then and had moved away from the farm. Though her own grown children continued to visit as often as possible to help their mother with her chores, it fell to Perley, Helen and their kids - who lived the closest - to shoulder most of the burden. Sometimes, to Helen's annoyance, it seemed Perley put his mother's needs before those of his own family. For the most part, though, Helen and Elsie Jane got along well together and for many years formed a close-knit family.

As was often the case in the early 1900s, the husband had sole control over the family money. And in Perley's eyes money was to be spent only on absolute necessities, not for entertainment or pleasure. Hard work would bring its proper rewards. And work they all did. Perley would justify his philosophy this way: *"All my work and everything I done I was trying my best to help the boys and girls both so they would have an easier and better life than mine was."* As a result, every extra penny was put aside for future land purchases.

Opting to spend money on necessities rather than niceties, Perley would show his affection for his family in ways that he felt were more practical, ways that would ease their workload. As his mother described in a letter, *"He fixed up a bathroom and sent off for a nice bathtub. He done the work himself. Digging the ditches and putting in the pipes. He also put in pipes so the water came to the sink in the kitchen by turning a faucet. He also had a hose pipe hanging in the cellar way that they could take to the stove and fill the tea kettle and anything else they wanted to, which made it very handy by saving steps. Later he bought a washing machine that run by gasoline power that cost over a hundred dollars. He was always good to get anything she [Helen] wanted. I think she had more to do with than most farmer's wives had."*

Yet at the same time, Perley did not consult his wife about his investments. He shared more information about such things with his mother than he did with Helen, a habit which began to create a distance between the two women. When Perley bought the 152-acre Fifield farm next door without telling her, Helen had just about reached the limit of her patience.

After receiving a tax bill for the Fifield property which he deemed extravagant, Perley, characteristically, complained to the town tax collector that the property wasn't worth what it was assessed for. Countering Perley's argument with one of his own, the tax collector turned the tables, saying that because the assessment was based on what Perley had paid for the land and because *"you are such a good judge of value and wouldn't pay more than it was worth, we must go by your judgment."* Even Perley couldn't argue with that reasoning.

In 1924, when her building project was in full swing, Florence Brooks-Aten turned its supervision over to Perley and her hired laborers in order to embark on another time-consuming and expensive venture. Ever the dreamer, and believing that her philanthropy could produce a better world, Florence started the Brooks-Bright Foundation (named after her great-great-grandfather, David Brooks, who fought with Washington in the War for Independence, and John Bright, a British politician and "one of the greatest orators of his generation.") The mission of this charitable organization was explained by Mrs. Aten in a letter (courtesy of the Arthur and Elizabeth Schlesinger Library, Cambridge, MA) she wrote to Fannie Fern Andrews of Boston, Massachusetts, a well-known lecturer on education in Europe and America and author of several published works on world relations: *"Having seen the late war at close range and having had a son in it, it has been brought home to me how horrible and useless war really is. For several years after its cessation I thought and consulted with others to find out in what way I could devote myself most efficiently to endeavor to prevent a recurrence. Thus, after mature thought and advice I came to the conclusion that the most practical way of accomplishing this was to have the two great English speaking nations stand together and act in amity and friendship and with mutual accord in international affairs. For them to do this requires a complete understanding between them."*

To achieve this goal of "complete understanding" between America and England, Florence felt it best to reach out to the children of both countries. Her philosophy was that, *"the boys and girls now in schools will determine the policies of tomorrow."* Toward this end, Florence's newly formed foundation sent out six thousand invitations offering students the opportunity to participate in an essay contest discussing the benefits of a friendly relationship between the two countries. The student who wrote the winning essay would receive for his school a replica in silver of an 1801 Old English loving cup which had belonged to David Brooks. The student author, himself, would win a miniature replica of the cup in gold. During the first year the Foundation received four hundred entries to the essay contest.

Florence's development of the Brooks-Bright Foundation was so efficient that she secured immediately the active cooperation of many prominent men and women of the United States of America and Great Britain. The Brooks-Bright Foundation made almost unprecedented strides and became a vital force in bringing the two countries together in friendship and understanding. Florence received many letters of commendation from prominent people, including ex-Presidents William H. Taft and Calvin Coolidge, Premier Mussolini of Italy and ex-Kaiser Wilhelm of Germany.

In managing her new foundation, Florence did not skimp on the amenities. She set up a fully furnished luxurious apartment in New York City complete with a private office, tea alcove and lounge as a meeting place for the directors of her new non-profit venture. Money not being a concern, history records that Florence also contributed $25,000 to the Yale University Library during this same time period.

The list of distinguished trustees of Florence's foundation grew quickly. University presidents sat on her board of directors as did many highly educated people from the most respected universities of the time including Yale, Harvard, and Princeton.

One such distinguished trustee was Dr. Charles Eastman, (no relation to the Eastmans of Rochester) the first American

Indian to achieve national and international distinction as an outstanding advocate of two civilizations. Eastman's Indian name was Ohiyesa and he was a Dakota Santee Sioux born in 1858 near Redwood Falls, Minnesota. His mother died shortly after his birth and for the first fifteen years of his life he lived the nomadic life of the Sioux with his father's Indian relatives. At that point, his father, who Charles had thought was dead, found him and took him into the white man's world, schooling him at Kimball Union Academy and Dartmouth College, both in New Hampshire. He subsequently moved on to Boston University where he earned his M.D. degree.

Dr. Eastman became renowned not only in the medical field but as an author of several books on Indian folklore as well. Possibly, Florence had become acquainted with Dr. Eastman when he and his wife ran a girl's summer camp, called Camp Oahe, at the three-mile distant Granite Lake in Munsonville, New Hampshire from 1915 to 1920. Mrs. Aten enlisted Dr. Eastman to travel to England to lecture on behalf of her Brooks-Bright Foundation.

Florence soon found, however, that she was stretching herself too thin, emotionally and financially, trying to keep up with all of her grand plans. *"I found that it* [the Brooks-Bright Foundation] *was decidedly more of a task and took much more time than I had any idea in organizing a movement such as this."* Florence wrote again to Mrs. Andrews: *"While I have kept no accurate record of my expenditures, I find in going over my accounts, that the movement to date has cost me in excess of a hundred thousand dollars, and it has been necessary for me to borrow in order to do this."* [letter courtesy of Schlesinger Library]

Florence found it increasingly difficult to manage her foundation in New York City and oversee on-site the development of her land in Stoddard. Unable to find the time to visit the area in person, she kept in contact with Perley through letters, asking him for details on the progression of the work being done on her behalf and giving him instructions on jobs she wanted him to do. *"Did you get the rest of that waterfront filled with sod and earth?"* she asked in one of many letters, *"And have you raked the leaves off the grass around the houses? It should be well manured and please don't forget to cover the roses, peonies, phlox and chrysanthemums up with a thick covering of spruce boughs."*

Similar to what Perley would experience in the coming years, Florence began to have legal problems. In 1925, George de Forest Brush, a well-known artist and part-time resident of Dublin, New Hampshire, was commissioned by Florence to paint a portrait of her which would be suitable for display in her lodge and used for publication in circulars to be distributed on behalf of her Brooks-Bright Foundation.

George de Forest Brush had made a name for himself, not only for his beautiful portraits but for his work in developing camouflage for the military. George was friendly with another member of the Dublin Art Colony, his neighbor, Abbott H. Thayer. Together they had collaborated on the use of "protective coloration," a form of military camouflage for American ships during the Spanish-American War. Their experiments in camouflage continued into World War I, both collaboratively and separately. Brush developed what was called a "transparent airplane" based on the coloration of a seagull.

Florence and George de Forest Brush agreed on a fee of $10,000 for her portrait, an exorbitant fee for that time even by a celebrated artist. When after ten sittings the completed portrait was presented, Mrs. Aten paid the fee but commented about the painting that the *"coloring is magnificent and the face so beautiful - but it doesn't look like me. Besides, the left arm is out of the drawing and the right hand is too stubby -*

fingers too short. I think you have painted a fine work but not my portrait." She also complained to Mr. Brush that the picture gave the impression she weighed 250 pounds which she wanted to be clear was definitely not the case. Finally, she felt that the cows he had painted into the background were quite inappropriate. Hardly concealing her displeasure she asked the famous artist, *"Won't you please touch it up, I would give anything for a good portrait."* We do not know how the artist received her criticisms of his work. But he did agree to rework the portrait although the requested changes went far beyond a mere "touch up." When the portrait was again finished he presented it to Florence with a bill for an additional $7,000. Of course, Florence balked at this extra fee and refused to pay. Painter De Forest Brush promptly sued.

After the first trial, Mr. Brush was awarded a reduced verdict of $4,000 of his original claim for $7,000. Still not happy, Florence took the case back to court two more times, with the final New York Supreme Court decision handed down in 1930 awarding Mr. Brush a settlement of $1,750. With hard times about to descend on Florence, it is unlikely Mr. Brush received any further payment. The painting simply disappeared and was forgotten until it resurfaced almost eighty years later through an amazing series of coincidences. (See "A Final Visit")

At the time when Florence began her acquaintance with artist Brush, Helen discovered that despite her attempts to practice birth control, she was pregnant once again. Her last child, Bernice Eva, was born March 17, 1928. And Perley, happy at having another addition to the family, was overjoyed that he had another daughter to love. (Their youngest son, Maurice, recalled later in life that the only time he ever remembered his father telling the children to "*go outside and play*" was when his mother was delivering his baby sister.) Of this last birth, Perley wrote:

*"Past troubles were all forgotten, when the last
    little girl had come,
  and the sins of the wife, if not forgiven, had greatly
    begun to fade;
She after many objections, gave it the father's choice
    of name,
  and another channel for his love, now to the man
    had been made."*

So Perley had his last little girl on whom to shower unspent affection. Though maybe not the perfect future Perley had once envisioned, he seemed reasonably content with his family, job and life in general.

Unfortunately, the future had a few more surprises in store for Perley and Helen...and Florence. Before too long disastrous events would overtake them, spinning their lives out of control.

Stone powerhouse with waterwheel
Built around 1925 by Florence Brooks Aten
Courtesy of Don and Joyce Healy

Rebuilt dam on Chandler Meadow pond on Florence's estate
Taken around 1930

Woods Mill house and barn in Stoddard, NH
Taken 1909

Chapter Eight
The End of a Dream

As the gulf in her relationship with Perley continued to widen, Helen grew to understand that what her father did to her many years before was not her fault and neither should she have to spend her entire life trying to atone for it. Whatever her thoughts on the matter were, she also began to take a stand against Perley's authority as the sole head of household. This was evidenced in a note she wrote to him stating that she didn't *"believe it is considered necessary that the father's word is law nowadays about everything, the wife and children have some rights."* Perley, in turn, was not happy to see this growing streak of independence in Helen.

A battle had been brewing over whether their three sons should stay in school and get their high school diplomas or drop out to help their father cut and sell the pine timber off their land. It was Perley's opinion that while the economy was good, and there was money to be made, the boys should put off their education for a few years. He had made exactly that same sacrifice for his parents and could not understand why his boys shouldn't do the same.

"You know how I feel about that!" Helen shouted back at Perley during one of their many 'discussions.' *"If the boys quit high school now they will never go back."*

Helen wanted her sons to be educated and have a chance at an easier life than that of a farmer. With a high school diploma she hoped more opportunities would be available to her boys as well as her girls. *"You can give the children money and land and they can lose it,"* she told Perley, *"but if you give them an education, that is something they will always have!"*

Perley wanted the same prosperity for his children that Helen did, but he felt there was a better way to achieve it. There was a building boom at the time and the demand for lumber was high. In 1928, while the economy was strong, Perley wanted to take advantage of this by supplying timber to the local sawmills. He felt there was a fortune to be made. But the work was strenuous and time-consuming and he would need all of his boys to work with him full-time to meet the demand.

Perley was also riding high on his land investments. He did not want to lose this window of opportunity to acquire still more land. He also needed to be sure he had enough cash on hand to pay real estate taxes when they came due. With his master plan, he felt he would be leaving a more valuable legacy to his children than a diploma would provide. In Perley's opinion this only meant the boys would be putting off their education for a year or two, with no harm done. However, his sons did not want to do this and Helen stood firmly behind them. The last thing the boys wanted was to leave school - for it was a place where they could escape from the depressing state of affairs at home - to work under their father's thumb.

Tempers flared and bitter sentiments were voiced, but in the end Helen and the boys won the battle. Perley gave in, causing even more resentment between Perley and Helen and driving a further wedge between Perley and his sons. Perley regarded his family's defiance not simply as a difference of opinion but more seriously...an act of treason that he could not easily forgive.

Perley

During the next few years when finances were tight, Perley would remonstrate with Helen: "*I wanted to cut pine and get some money again in the bank for a reserve to pay taxes and insurance, but you would not let the boys help. You sent them to high school against my advice, when I told you we could not afford it then. I never expected what came,* [the Depression] *but I did know there would not always be a chance to get four to five dollars a day in this neighborhood for our work and an education is not worth it got at that cost.*"

With the weight of his land investments squarely on his own shoulders, and facing the Great Depression, Perley withdrew further into his own thoughts. And as he was prone to do at such times, he expressed those deepest thoughts poetically. The following lament he titled, "The Cost of Education:"

We seemed to be happy in the bye gone days,
 And found money to fill all our needs;
Till wife and boys got the education craze,
 I know not who first sowed the seeds.

The money it then had to come from the bank,
 What the boys had saved up for their start;
It soon was all gone and their mother sank,
 Her lifetime savings, or at least the bigger part.

Times were at first good and wages were high,
 But I needed help the boys might have gave;
Chances to make money I had to let go by,
 Now I am broke and headed for the grave.

Dull now are the times and work is not found,
 They could have gone to school now well as not;

The End of a Dream

And had money in plenty and no one be bound,
By debts that can never be paid or forgot.

On December 1st of 1928, nine months after Helen's last child was born, Helen's mother, Emma added fuel to the family fire when she came to stay with the Swett family. In the past, Emma had come and gone, staying with Helen to help when each new baby was born. Usually she came without Perley's knowledge or consent and her treatment of him at those times ranged from mere tolerance to downright nastiness. *"Each time she came she seemed to get more bossy and disagreeable,"* said Elsie Jane. Emma, on the other hand, may have been angry at Perley for insisting that her daughter continue to produce children at the expense of her health.

Over the years of their marriage, Helen and Perley had seldom shared the same bedroom. Helen did not like to sleep through the night with him, insisting she could only get her rest if she slept alone. Though Perley tried many times over the years to convince her otherwise, as he liked to have her beside him as he slept, she always insisted on keeping separate sleeping arrangements. Perley was forced to sleep in the upstairs hallway on a cot. While Helen regularly allowed Perley to visit her bed at night, she then insisted he return to his cot to sleep. Though Perley was not pleased with this arrangement, he grudgingly accepted it.

Now, however, whether as a conspiracy between them or for convenience sake, Emma had set up her sleeping arrangements in the room beside Helen's...a room that shared a doorway that was always left open. Using her mother's proximity as a convenient excuse, Helen refused to allow Perley into her bed at night. If he tried to climb into her bed, she had the twins forcibly drive him back upstairs.

This last pregnancy had been a mistake and Helen was through taking chances. Furthermore, her health had deteriorated. Always a hard worker, the added marital stress, seven births and caring for six surviving children had taken a toll on her body. At the age of forty-two, she found she no longer had the energy she once had and spent days at a time lying on the daybed just off the kitchen. She may have been suffering from illness and, most likely, depression.

Their marriage had devolved into a continuing series of related conflicts. And no longer was there any room for discussion or negotiation as each had taken a hard line. Perley still felt he needed more help on the farm and wanted more children...

> *The children came till we now have six, twice as many*
> *would not make me stop;*
> *But my wife either knew or learned modern tricks,*
> *so any prospect of a new record had to drop.*

Helen had nearly died in childbirth and Perley was talking about breaking records! Fear of pregnancy was probably not the only reason Helen had for refusing to sleep with Perley.

In the days, weeks and months that followed, with no sign of Emma leaving or of Helen allowing him into her bed, Perley's anger and frustration grew. In retaliation, he tried the tactic that his own father had often used; he stopped talking to Helen in the hopes that she would see the "error of her ways" and become "a true wife" to him again. Considering the lack of communication that normally existed between Perley and Helen, the silent treatment hardly made a difference. After years of listening to Perley's criticisms, a little peace and quiet was a welcome change.

When Perley did deign to speak to Helen it was to threaten that "*if things don't change around here I'm leav-*

ing." After hearing this again and again her reply was, *"why don't you just go instead of talking about it so much."*

A friend of the twins who visited during this time recalled that everyone in the family seemed quite somber. *"There was no happiness in that house,"* she said. The family continued to flounder in anger, resentment and lack of communication for the next two years. Add to that the gloom cast by the onset of the Great Depression and it was a recipe for disaster.

* * *

At that time, Florence's dream a mile away at Wood's Mill was similarly headed for ruin. The rumor about town had been that the rich philanthropist from New York *"could not spend all her income, no matter how hard she tried,"* although it certainly seemed that Mrs. Aten was trying. Her "simple life" had come with a hefty price tag.

To her credit, Florence was a woman of both taste and unusual generosity. Rather than try to cut back on her philanthropies her list of donations seemed to be growing steadily. At a time when she had more than enough on her plate, Florence was unable to say "no" to any charity or group seeking money. In addition to her work on the Brooks-Bright foundation, she gave $25,000 to the Yale University Library, she gave out several Princeton scholarships, a donation of $3,000 for an exterior pulpit at Princeton University, she paid the full college tuition for several needy students, and she even paid for the entire regatta crew from Cambridge to compete in the Henley Regatta in England. Florence felt obligated to also take over the work of her grandfather in donating thousands of dollars to the renovation of a small church in Germany where her great-grandfather was buried. Locally, Florence contributed generously to the Elliot

Community Hospital. In recognition of her large donations she was named to the board of incorporators.

Though by 1928 Florence was strapped to the breaking point, she could not turn her back on poor Dora Bumford, the woman who died in the Blizzard of 1888 and was buried in what was meant to be a temporary grave in a sandbank at Wood's Mill. Florence felt that Dora should be moved to a more appropriate location and she had the body exhumed and re-buried in the Old Cemetery in Stoddard Center village. Florence had a gravestone erected that reads: "Dora C. Bumford, born in Unity, died in Stoddard, March 1888."

With the extravagant disposition of one born into wealth, Florence shared her fortune willingly. While her ambitions were noble, her pursuit of them was naïve. She placed a great deal of trust in others, especially when it came to the management of her own finances. Her family fortune was fully invested in the stock market, much of it on margin, during the postwar boom of the mid-1920s. She was accustomed to the substantial income her portfolio produced and oblivious to the warning signs that change was coming. Instead, Florence continued to spend up to her income, and beyond, on building her Wood's Mill estate and on her charitable endeavors, confident that her financial future was secure.

Until October 12, 1929 - Black Tuesday - when she lost everything. Many rich people became poor people in one single day. Florence Brooks-Aten was, indeed, one of them.

Not only were her dreams for her "Utopia" utterly shattered but those who depended on Mrs. Aten for their employment were also deeply affected. Suddenly Perley and many other local craftsmen found themselves out of work at a time when there were few jobs to be had. In Mrs. Aten's own words, *"It does seem little less than a tragedy that my financial losses have been the cause of bringing about such a condition in the lives of others as well as my having to give up my own home to which I gave the best part of my life, as well as money, to the winding trail that led to home sweet home down between the hills and waters of old Wood's Mill."*

Ironically, the poor farmers who had been living a life of subsistence off their lands were probably those least affected by the Great Depression. They were conditioned to doing without and could sustain themselves with what their farms produced. Though losing his job created a financial hardship for Perley and his family, they still had a roof over their heads and food on their table.

Florence's plans for completing her estate at Wood's Mill and endowing the Brooks-Bright Foundation collapsed along with the stock market. She had already spent between a quarter and a half million dollars according to local estimates, overpaying for labor and materials to many who took advantage of her wealth and trust. It was said that she still owed almost $17,000 to local vendors (the amount may well have been much higher). Those who had been quite willing to extend her credit when times were good now demanded payment, seeking redress through the courts.

The Brooks-Bright Foundation, which had shown such promise and enjoyed enthusiastic support from a distinguished board, found itself unable to pay its bills. Florence had no choice but to shut it down. She stoically explained her situation to her board of directors in a letter (Courtesy of the Schlesinger Library) dated December 29, 1930: *"First I wish to state with the utmost emphasis that I am not a poor, unfortunate woman who has been imposed upon and through improper guidance has had her estate wiped out. What I gave I gave gladly and I was fully aware at all times of my position and my risks. Nor have I the slightest regret for one penny that I paid out for this movement. I found a greater happiness and joy in doing it than anything I have ever done."*

A proud woman, she was still attempting to put a good face on her misfortune. Unfortunately, none of the people or institutions who had benefited by her gifts of several hundred thousand dollars when she was wealthy, had come forward to help her in her hour of need. Instead, Florence was considering taking a job in a cotton mill for ten dollars a week.

As time went on it was becoming clear that stress was taking a terrible toll on Florence's health, both mentally and physically. She despairingly wrote to Elsie Jane: *"There is no one who will give me a hand. I have exhausted even my personal belongings, even my clothing; some of it I sold last winter. Slippers, dresses, opera coats, furs, and all are gone."* And, *"I haven't been well. I have a bad heart and low blood pressure. I am sick and tired of the whole thing."*

For the next few years, Florence's estate was held by the court as her creditors fought over her assets. *"I haven't a home now. The apartment in New York is gone and everything I had was sold to pay my debts."* In a letter to Perley she admitted, *"I have only myself to blame for having undertaken the project of attempting to make something worthwhile of a property that was more than any woman alone should have attempted to undertake. The losses sustained by me were of unbelievable proportions and I have been paying in more ways than money for the losses ever since. No lamb, sheep, goat 'n dog was fleeced more closely than 'Mrs. Aten' in those days of 'Fleece the Rich.'"*

Though Florence had accepted some responsibility for her problems, she still blamed others. She became bitter about the way she was being treated by her former workers, especially her architect, Augustus Shepard, about whom she complained to Perley, *"I am so disgusted with the whole works connected with Shepard that I don't know how to express it. Curse words won't do it and a bomb dropped on his head would do so better! If that Shepard man had been square the whole situation would have been saved!"*

Florence could no longer think rationally. Her dreams had been shattered, she had abandoned hope and knew that in the end, nothing would be saved.

Wood's Mill had lost its visionary. And the same was about to happen at the Swett homestead one mile north on Taylor Pond.

Florence Brooks Aten in front of
Shinbone Shack - Taken around 1925

Chapter Nine
It All Comes Crashing Down

On September 15, 1930, after almost two years of listening to his mother-in-law's carping and his bed still empty, Perley could take no more. In protest, he moved out of the home that meant so much to him. Taking a few meager belongings, Perley set himself up in the Fifield house next door which he had bought a few years earlier. It was only a few minutes walk from his home but this was Perley's way of making a statement about how unhappy and frustrated he was. He expected this move would be temporary since his family would be so distraught at his leaving that they would beg him to return.

Perley kept their meager lines of communication open by writing letters to his wife by way of the twins. Though at this time Perley and Helen were both in their early forties, their correspondence reads like it was written by a pair of pouting teenagers, with neither one willing to give an inch.

Perley still worried that Helen didn't have feelings for him and was looking for proof otherwise. *"Have found you don't miss me any,"* he wrote, *"and think now you were trying to get rid of me as I told you I could not stay there as things were going."* She deeply resented his moodiness and chose to play dumb about the situation that had led to his leaving. *"You always fuss so about everything,"* Helen replied, *"that I don't know just the reasons you left."*

Ironically, Perley and Helen did care for each other but neither knew how to repair their damaged relationship. Together they had spent twenty years building farm, family and future. Each wanted desperately to know that the other understood the pain each was going through. Somehow, their troubled marriage had survived the wounds of Helen's incest and supposed affair with Arthur Aten, of Perley's incessant demands for proof of Helen's affection, along with his desire for more children and arguments over the boys' schooling. But those deep wounds had left scars. Helen needed to find peace. Perley needed to find love...love which possibly Helen did not and never did have for him. And after twenty years of dueling, their differences were becoming irreconcilable.

Still concerned with his wellbeing, Helen sent the children next door with food and clean clothes for Perley. What he wanted most, of course, was for her to come herself, full of apologies and promises that she would become a "true wife" to him again if he moved back home.

The house he had moved to was empty and cold. There was very little furniture and no sweet comforts of home. He missed the hubbub from his children's activities. And as a father figure, it was not his way to desert his family. But Perley had his own requirements for returning home and his pride would not allow him to be the first one to give in! Surprisingly, shortly after he moved out, Helen's mother also left, adding credence to Perley's belief that Helen and her mother had conspired to break up the marriage.

Alone and distraught, Perley returned to his poetry on those quiet evenings to express his troubled feelings. Most of his poems reeked of self-pity, expressing the pain and disappointment in his life. Living apart, both he and Helen continued to harden their positions.

At first Perley paid his family's expenses. But in time, when he could see that they were getting along fine without him, and realizing that the children were siding with their mother, he angrily refused to support them. Perley reasoned that there were three able-bodied teenage boys living on 'his' farm, tax and rent-free, with all his stock and tools. Why should he be expected to support them all when he no longer had ready access to the means for earning an income. Feeling rejected by his family, his anger and resentment grew. Incredibly this situation lasted for almost two more years while Perley and Helen continued their bickering from a distance. Perley's youngest daughter barely remembered seeing him during this time.

With no financial support from Perley, Helen's situation was becoming intolerable. It was very draining caring for a big home and holding the family together. Her only income came from doing laundry for neighbors, selling vegetables and berries in town and doing a little mending for hire. Helen felt, and rightly so, that Perley should be contributing toward the care of his family. While he had never shared his financial situation with her, she assumed that he had cash in his bank account. She could not understand why he would desert his family and refuse to contribute to their support. Finally, when Helen sent the twins to Perley to ask for money for new shoes and they came back empty-handed, Helen decided to take action. She had the local sheriff arrest him for non-support of his family.

Perley was dumbfounded that she would do such a thing. Not only was it a public blow to his pride, he reasoned that since he had no way to earn a living, (this was at the height of the Depression) was unable to work his own farm, and had no cash on hand, he should not be expected to pay money for a family that lived free of charge in his house and on his land.

Perley was distraught. The case was brought to court and during the proceedings the judge asked Helen how much she felt she would need to *"support yourself and three daughters a week.*" She thought for a moment and replied, *"Five or six dollars should be enough."* Not thinking he heard correctly, finding the sum even then too low, he asked Helen to repeat herself. The judge finally settled on $8.00 a week for Perley to pay for child support.

Though $8.00 a week seems like a paltry sum to support a family, in 1932 it seemed like an incredible amount to Perley. He tried for a while to pay the court ordered support but with the Depression in full swing, there was little way to earn money and he soon fell into arrears.

Perley was becoming increasingly infuriated with his circumstances. He resented the fact that most of his own brothers and sisters and neighbors all sided with Helen. "By appearance I guess folks think I am a rather low down sort of person to 'desert' my wife and children but as much as I thought of my home and family I would never have left except as a last resort."

Accepting the fact that it was unlikely that they would ever be able to live as husband and wife again, Perley and Helen began to talk about divorce. They tried to reach a just settlement but neither could agree on what was fair. Cash was not the issue. Ironically, it was due to Perley's strategy of investing in property that now gave them so much to fight over.

In the meantime, taxes were coming due. Whether to save his property from being sold at tax auctions or in an attempt to keep it from falling into Helen's hands, Perley deeded almost all of his property to his mother. In Perley's mind it didn't matter that Helen had worked side by side with him for twenty years helping to build their equity. Because he had earned the money and bought the land, he considered all the property they owned was his to do with as he saw fit. As always, Elsie Jane firmly supported Perley. When Helen realized what he had done, she was livid. She could imagine

Perley and his mother conspiring to leave her with nothing. She took Perley back to court for non-support.

Helen's lawyer was also the District Attorney and he was determined that Perley pay Helen all that was due to her. Perley could hardly afford the extra expense but he realized that now he also needed a lawyer to defend his interests. He had not yet developed the deep distrust of lawyers that would grow through the remaining years of his life. At this point he still held a slim hope that some compromise could be found and that he would be able to move back home to his farm and family. A divorce was never what Perley wanted. But stubborn pride again would keep him from making a move toward reconciliation.

From the start, Perley clashed with his lawyer. He felt that he knew best, never realizing that when his lawyer advised him to do something contrary to his wishes, it might actually be for his own good. Also, due to the remote location of Perley's home and lack of transportation, it was very difficult for him to communicate with his lawyer. As a result, his case floundered. (Subsequently, Perley earned a reputation among those in the local legal profession of being a very difficult client, making it challenging for him to find someone to represent him in future legal battles.)

Elsie Jane was now dragged into the divorce proceedings by Helen's lawyer who saw her as an accomplice to Perley. Having been deeded most of Perley's property and having bought the rest through tax sales, Elsie Jane now owned all of it. Helen's lawyers quickly put an attachment on everything Elsie Jane owned so she was unable to sell or even work the land as she chose. The attorneys tried to hammer out a settlement but no agreement could be reached. Helen insisted on being awarded the home farm along with other parcels of property as well as custody of the children. Remembering his suspicions about the circumstances of his young son's death,

Perley was loathe to turn over total custody of his youngest daughter to Helen. He expressed his fear in a letter to his lawyer: *"I dared not trust her to spend a good share of 'alimony and support' money to raise a small child she never wanted to have when it could be buried for less than one tenth the cost of raising it."* Perley also refused to give up the home that he had purchased before he even turned twenty-one. They were at a stalemate. As his lawyer rather candidly summed it up, *"the whole business is a complicated mess."*

Finally on Dec. 26, 1933 the judge handed down his ruling: Helen would receive the home farm she and the children were living on along with two pasture lands adjoining it, and all the livestock and farm equipment, or be paid the sum of $3,000 in lieu of any land. Perley was between a rock and a hard place. On one hand he had no cash. On the other he could not bear the thought of parting with his beloved farm, which was now in his mother's name. It was time to change strategy.

"I am tired of posing as a base sinner," Perley wrote to Helen, *"with you taking the role of an abused angel."* Perley felt railroaded and cheated by the court system and now threatened Helen with revealing everything if she tried to force him into *"accepting forced terms."* Up until this point Perley had tried to spare Helen (and himself) the embarrassment of having her past known to the whole town. But he now decided he had to play that card. Perley had convinced himself that if he had a chance to tell his side of the story, informing the judge about Helen's sordid past, the judge would have no choice but to find in his favor.

And Helen realized that Perley had no intention of turning anything over to her in compliance with the judge's orders. So she was determined to force him into living up to the court settlement whether he divulged secrets of her past life or not.

After numerous legal wranglings and the judge's refusal to consider Perley's testimony about Helen's misdeeds, deeming it irrelevant, the divorce was finally granted in March 1934. *"It seems like a bad dream or nightmare these last three years,"* Perley wrote to Helen, still adding wistfully, *"only I never wake to find you beside me..."*

Perley was more convinced than ever that he was the victim of an unjust court system that was attempting to impoverish him. In one sentence he summed up his plight. *"Five years ago,"* he wrote, *"I considered there were not a dozen men in town better off financially than I and now I am nearly, if not quite, at the very bottom of the list."* So he felt he had to fight for what he thought were his rights, and refused to comply with the judge's decision.

As a result, the judge declared the deed from Perley to his mother fraudulent and insisted Perley give Helen either the property or the money demanded by the court. Perley countered that he had no money and also no longer owned any property and, therefore, could deed nothing to Helen.

In the meantime, Helen's lawyer sent a letter to the judge asking that Perley be found guilty of contempt of court and that this case be settled once and for all. The judge agreed and the sheriff was directed to take Perley to the County Farm where he would remain until he was willing to turn over either property or money to Helen. The judge and Helen's lawyer undoubtedly thought that when faced with actual jail time Perley would finally relent. No one could foresee how stubborn Perley would become when he believed he was in the right.

During this time, Florence Aten was in the midst of litigation to save her own land. As with Perley, her's would be a losing battle. Though she had fought hard to hold on to it, Florence's woodland estate and the twelve hundred acres surrounding it, valued at more than $200,000 in 1934, was finally sold at auction for a mere $9,800, with all the money going to creditors.

For the next few years, as Perley languished behind bars, Florence was experiencing her own form of imprisonment. No longer a socialite, she sometimes lived off friends or relatives, at another time renting a tiny upstairs room in New York City.

"I am thankful for a clean bed and enough to eat," Florence wrote to Elsie Jane, *"but I've sold everything I could turn into a nickel and am living on the proceeds. The city is so expensive and my room is on the 3rd floor and cold. I can live on less than $1.00 a day by buying cheap and cooking for myself in a bathroom where I have a two burner electric stove. I eat very little and need little."*

Before she lost her money Florence had been sending her son, Albert, $400 a month to supplement his own income. Now she only heard from him once a year on her birthday when he would send her $20. *"Even Albert takes my loss unkindly."*

Florence was desperate to escape New York. *"I want so much to go to the country and never come back to the city again,"* she wrote, *"I never knew sickness all the years I was there* [in New Hampshire] *and I haven't known a well day since I came to the city. The crowded streets I dislike and only live from day to day and seldom see anyone. No inmate of Alcatraz prison could be more shut in."* Once a celebrated philanthropist, she was now quite alone. *"Those people who came fawning around me when I had money were not my friends, they would not look at me today."*

Florence continued to write to Elsie Jane, her letters filled with self-pity, lamenting how much she missed *"my dear home down there in a dell, my ferns and rocks I love so well, each stick, tree, fern and rock I can see them as if I were there. The wild rose bush where the robins came and built their home and stay each year and sang for me their sweetest songs. Oh, it is hard to feel it is no longer there for me. I worked so hard to finish up and wanted to plant apple trees, willows along the banks across the way, to have a vegetable and flower garden, a pretty fountain when the birds would come and to have at last the end of the working and to then be there always till I died. But God ordained it not to be. I have it seems always lost what I most loved and lost faith in those I put my trust."*

It is very likely that Perley - consumed also by self-pity - was thinking these same sentiments as he contemplated the course his life had taken. And he had plenty of time to think, for his stubbornness would keep him in jail for the next three years. On principle, he might have been willing to stay there until he died, but, fortunately for him, his ex-wife Helen beat him to it.

Perley Swett with his twins, Dora and Dorothy Swett
Taken around 1924

Chapter Ten
A Prideful Incarceration

In the mid 1800s it became necessary for many small towns to establish a facility variously known as an asylum, a poorhouse and more kindly, a "County Farm." It came about as a result of a reform movement to provide better care for society's downtrodden, those who were mentally ill, aged or disabled who had no way to support themselves or a family willing to provide for them. Previously town officials auctioned off these poor souls in return for a year's worth of labor. If the person was unable to work, the town paid the *lowest* bidder for his or her keep. *"The bidder contracted to keep the person or persons for a year's time. When the year was up, another auction would be held and another contract negotiated."* (The History and Genealogy of Westmoreland, NH)

Because of the lack of proper care that these paupers received, this method of looking after society's outcasts was called to question. The answer was to build a more easily supervised institution where the individuals, and whole families when necessary, could be cared for. In turn, responsible citizens were not subjected to the *"threat of idle and criminal elements in its population."*

A county poorhouse was built near the Connecticut River in the town of Westmoreland, New Hampshire, in 1868. From its inception the County Farm housed *"several different classes of inmates."* It was an orphanage for children as young as one year old; a yard was fenced off for use by the insane; and the poor, elderly and disabled who had no means of support were also residents.

In 1875 its use was further expanded. A portion of the farm was set aside as a House of Corrections. In that first year fifty-three men were committed, the majority for minor infractions.

It was to this facility that Perley Edwin Swett was sent, and on May 18, 1934 the doors shut on Perley's freedom. Perley was devastated. He was a man of high principles, a man of honor whose word could be trusted. Wronged by the judicial system (in his opinion) and being thought of as a convict was a terrible blow to his self esteem, a final humiliation. He still could not see any wrongdoing on his part as evidenced by this portion of a letter he wrote to his twin daughters: *"I can only say I will have a little satisfaction in knowing I fought fair and am still honest after a year among criminals."* The "criminals" he was referring to were the lawyers, Helen's witnesses, and the judge who Perley felt had all lied and conspired to put him behind bars. It gave him a distrust and resentment of the legal system that would last for the rest of his life.

Most inmates sent to the County Farm were detained due to drunkenness. Upon arrest they were allowed to sleep off their spirits, do a few days work, and then be released. Other detentions were for crimes such as driving an unregistered vehicle, committing adultery, selling or possessing liquor and disturbing the peace. More serious charges included larceny and destruction of property, but dangerous criminals convicted of more violent crimes were sent to a state prison. Convicted of lesser crimes, the majority of inmates at the County Farm in Westmoreland were held for no more than two to three months. Unfortunately, Perley would prove to be an exception to this rule.

Perley immediately began to alienate himself from those in charge. He had never been one to accept the authority of others. Now he rebelled against all who held him against his will. In confrontations with his jailers and in a flood of correspondence sent to anyone who might listen, Perley railed against the *"conspiracy to defeat justice"* that he felt took place during his divorce trial. Though his complaints of injustice held little merit, Perley needed others to understand his pain. As might be expected, many grew to consider Perley as something of a joke. *"Is there such an offense in this state as 'contempt of clerk'?,"* the clerk of the court wrote to Judge James in complaint. *"I have heard of stuffing ballot boxes but if Swett keeps on writing, he should be in for 'stuffing the records'!"*

Though Perley continued to write to lawyers and anyone else who might help win his release, he seemed to accept his incarceration as a martyr accepts his fate. And Perley did regard himself as a martyr, someone whose beliefs were so grossly violated by those in authority that he resolved to never be coerced into submission. Ironically, Perley had "the keys to the jail" in his possession since it was within his power to gain his release at any moment if he simply agreed to the court's decree and gave Helen her rightful settlement. [Note: at that time the court could not mandate the settlement it had handed down to Perley and Helen as it did not have the legal authority to transfer ownership of property. Instead, the farm and land would have to be sold to the highest bidder at auction. That meant that Helen and the children would lose their home. Also the people most likely to have an interest in the farm were locals who did not want to become involved in their neighbor's business.]

Looking beyond the indignity he felt at being a "convict," Perley wrote to his mother that his initial introduction to the County Farm was not *"half as bad as* (he) *was expecting."* Perley actually got along well with the other prisoners, seeing them as allies in his fight against injustice. The Judge commented to one of the attorneys on the case: *"I think Perley probably likes the H of C. Its probably the best house he ever had!"*

The County Farm was a complex of buildings. There were barns and storage areas to house supplies and livestock. A large white house with black shutters and a spacious wraparound porch housed apartments for the Superintendent and his family. Next to the Super's house was a huge brick building with rooms where the prisoners and poor people were lodged.

Actual jail cells with bars were in the basement. They consisted of six small cubicles which held the more dangerous prisoners or those awaiting sentencing. These cells were sometimes used as places of punishment for the inmates needing to be *"taught a lesson."* These cells were dark, lacking windows and proper lighting. They were damp and cold, even in the summer, when the cement walls would sweat and create a musty, mildewed odor. It was a dismal place that Perley came to know well.

The majority of inmates serving time slept in one large dormitory type room upstairs. Filled with cots, there was no privacy. But at least this room had large windows, albeit barred, that could be opened to let in fresh air. This was where the prisoners spent the majority of their time when they did not have outside chores.

Inmates were expected to work off their sentences which enabled the farm to run smoothly and support itself. Their work days started early, especially those given the task of working in the dairy, where milking the cows began before breakfast. There were guards posted 24-hours a day. They had the duty to wake the prisoners in the mornings. After breakfast the entire prison population went to their assigned tasks.

The Farm consisted of a dairy, a piggery, a laundry, a boiler room and acres of gardens where inmates grew their own vegetables. Grain was raised and haying done in season to help feed the farm's livestock. The inmates kept swarms of bees for honey production. Lumber for building projects was cut and planed in the farm's own sawmill. There was also a hospital on the premises which provided medical care for the prisoners as well as town residents.

Those with the necessary skills were put to work on some type of repair or building project. Poor and destitute people staying in the almshouse often worked side by side with the prisoners. When the gardens were harvested, the women living there did the canning and preserving necessary to feed everyone during the winter months.

At lunch time work stopped and all gathered in the cafeteria to eat their meals together. Perley wrote to his mother that the food was *"good and sufficient (usually) but not enough time to eat it, especially for those with bad teeth."*

After lunch everyone returned to their chores. The work day usually ended at 5:00 pm unless a particular job, such as haying, required that the prisoners work later into the evening to finish. After supper was served, the inmates were locked in their common room for the night. Their time in the evenings was to be spent visiting quietly with other inmates, playing cards, writing letters or reading. Lights out came early. Visitation with family members was limited to Sundays from 9:00 am to 12:00 pm and Wednesday evenings from 6:00 to 8:00.

Though there were bars on the windows there were no fences or confinement of any kind around the grounds. If a prisoner had a mind to escape, it would be an easy feat. But because most of the prisoners held in the county farm were there for minor offenses and usually had only a short amount of time to serve, there was little concern that someone would risk extending their sentence by escaping. So, the days passed fairly smoothly for everyone. Or would have if Perley had been a less headstrong and persistent individual.

Unfortunately, Perley was not one to cooperate when under pressure. Cast into the role of martyr, he would play the part with great gusto, upstaging everyone else. Still determined to clear his name, he continued to send his letters to lawyer after lawyer. He was looking for one who would take his case and help him win back not simply his good name but also compensation along with an apology from the court for being "wrongfully" sent to prison. Fortunately, all the lawyers he contacted were frank enough to tell him the truth, which was that he didn't have a chance to win and that they chose not to represent him. As one attorney bluntly told him, *"It is my practice not to take cases unless I am of the opinion that I can do my clients some good. After reading the papers you sent me, I am of the opinion that I can do nothing for you."*

When Perley found his letters were producing no result, he vented his rising frustration via more immediate complaints. Never one to let a wrong go unnoticed, he appointed himself the watchdog of prisoners' rights at the county farm. Thus began a pattern of behavior that became a habit, challenging authority whenever he felt that he or his fellow inmates were being subjected to unjust treatment.

One such perceived injustice occurred on Sunday nights when *"crackers and milk were the bill of fare."* One of the main staples produced at the County Farm was milk and dairy products. The Farm produced over 200,000 pounds of milk a year. Perley's complaint was that the inmates were served *"separated,"* or skim, milk that was *"old and unfit to drink."*

Perley

Accustomed to drinking whole milk on his farm, he complained that the cream which should have been left in to flavor the inmates' milk was instead removed and added to milk that was sold to the public in order to make it richer. Accordingly, he circulated a petition to the other prisoners for their signatures and then sent it to several public officials. Perley couldn't understand why no one was willing to become involved in what he considered such an important issue. Once a coddled and favorite son and, later, a head of household, Perley - for the first time in his life - had been stripped of authority. It was a hard blow to his ego to realize he was just another inmate. All he really succeeded in doing in his fight for justice was to further alienate those in charge of his incarceration, and this was not a smart thing to do.

Only one small ray of sunshine found its way into the dark recesses of Perley's mind. Remarkably, he felt he had received some measure of understanding, some sign of *affection,* from an unlikely source. And that was Mrs. Sherman, the Superintendent's wife! Mrs. Sherman was a kind woman who treated all the prisoners with respect. Starved for affection from any quarter, and probably misinterpreting her general kindness as a deeper interest, Perley again turned to his poetry to express his feelings. The product of his introspections was a poem which he sent to Mrs. Sherman in which he returned her perceived affection. Though innocent in his mind, the consequence of his action, when the poem was read by the Superintendent, was immediate confinement in a 5'x7' cell in the 'dungeon' with a *"scant allowance"* of food. As Perley described that experience, the bread and water he was served *"was old and the cell was dirty and made me sick. The toilet bucket another had used for 5 or 6 days was not emptied till the fifth day I was there. Between the dirty mattress, this bucket and all, I did not eat or drink the 6 days I was in there. Was not even given a once over by a doctor but had to go out to the dining room with the others when I came out on the 6th day."*

Most of the men in jail with Perley were not well educated. With a comparatively quick mind and flair for the written word, Perley assumed the role of spokesman for his fellow inmates against the injustices he felt he and they suffered. Most of the other prisoners were in jail for only a short time and felt it was not in their best interests to create a fuss. But Perley had already been at the County Farm for more than a year, with no end in sight. Therefore he figured that if this was to be his future, he might as well try to make it as comfortable as possible. So following his continued plea for better milk, he also fought for better lighting, more time for meals and better sanitary conditions. And not simply concerned with his own comfort, Perley wrote to the Superintendent to ask that a fellow prisoner *"who suffers with bad eye sight and needs care for his eyes"* be released from solitary confinement so he could receive proper medical attention. Perley's philosophy had always been to *"aid the underdog in any just cause rather than being friends with the unjust."*

A so-called "payday" for the inmates came around once a week when they were given a measure of tobacco as an incentive for their work. Because Perley didn't use tobacco he felt he should be compensated with *"a few apples and oranges instead."* Those in charge didn't agree and again Perley threatened to contact a State Official and the press to make his grievances known.

By this time Perley's legalese was becoming quite proficient. Turning his former complaint about milk into a demand, one of his petitions read as follows:

"We, the undersigned prisoners and inmates at Cheshire County Farm, ask respectfully that you, as Superintendent of

this Institution may give the necessary orders (to your hired help and assistants) that will secure for the prisoners and inmates a reasonable amount of good, whole milk (not over twenty-four hours old), for Sundays and other nights when crackers or bread and milk is the main item on the bill of fare.

And we further ask that you give other orders to secure for the prisoners and also the inmates not less than twenty minutes time after the doors are opened to the dining room before they are closed or any one hastened about their meal.

The prisoners and inmates signing this petition feel these two requests are both reasonable and proper to ask and will be accepted by you in a friendly spirit and granted in full, without the necessity of saying or doing anything to cause bad feeling or causing this petition to be sent to some N.H. Paper or to a State Official."

To focus attention on his case, Perley also reached outside the institution. In a letter he wrote to the Boston Post, obviously looking for some attention, Perley questioned the newspaper: *"Just why did a man in a Vermont jail get a good write-up at least twice in your paper while a New Hampshire man* [Perley] *nearly twice that time in jail is still unknown and unhonored."*

As would be expected, Perley's letter writing and threats had turned the Superintendent and his staff against him. Other inmates, whenever possible, were given a choice of what type of work they might do. Perley made it well known that he preferred to work outdoors. Now he found himself punished, given chores only inside the barn and told that if he didn't work, he wouldn't eat. Furthermore, the *"Turnkey,"* the person in charge of work details, threatened to *"knock* [Perley's] *head off his shoulders"* if he saw him outside the barn.

Perley also felt that the Superintendent heaped more work on Perley in the hopes of breaking him. This caused him to resist even further, refusing to do what he felt was *"the work of two men."* As a result Perley was put on *"short rations with no dessert."* His meals now consisted of *"only a cup of tea, bowl of separator milk and 3 or 4 small crackers or slice of bread in place of crackers."* His weight dropped to 120 pounds. *"It has been scant rations, in fact an almost starvation diet."* Perley wrote to a frantic Elsie Jane; *"One small potato, gravy, one slice meat and small slice bread. One time only three crackers with a small allowance of pea soup."*

Perley described his punishment in verse:

"For failing to take on another man's work, beside all
he were able, and often more;
On very short rations three months he were kept, where his
bed took up half the floor,
Six full days he were in a damp, dirty dungeon, on a "bread
and water fare" confined;
The water stagnant, he neither ate or drank, nor promised
"official" orders to mind."

Perley was confined to solitary several times for even longer periods ranging from six weeks to almost five months. He would only be let out once every two weeks for a bath, a shave and for clean clothes. Now Perley's separation from society, both physically and emotionally, was becoming irreversible, driven by circumstances neither he nor his jailors were willing to change.

In a letter to his mother, the only person who still believed in him, Perley told her how one night he wandered too far from the prison, picking berries alone until dusk. Looking up into the evening sky he had thought wistfully of his home and family. For a short time that night he was able to forget he was a prisoner. Upon returning to the farm an hour late he was quickly reminded and harshly disciplined when he *"was yanked by the collar and slammed down on the cement stairway and put in without supper."*

As he later wrote to the Superintendent, *"Though you may keep me locked up or kill me, my pride is unbreakable!"* He had fully embraced martyrdom.

Cheshire County Farm, Westmoreland, NH

Cheshire County Farm corridor
Courtesy of Historical Society of Cheshire County

Chapter Eleven
Elsie Jane's Pain

Though Perley seemed resigned to the status quo of the county farm rather than give in to Helen, his mother was not willing to sit back and watch her favorite son languish behind bars for the rest of his life. Elsie Jane not only wanted him out of *"that awful place,"* but she also desperately needed his help at home to work the farm. She was seventy-five years old and struggling to manage several hundred acres with only a hired hand or two. Having Perley locked up was, in fact, placing an even heavier burden on her physically, emotionally and financially.

While Perley was incarcerated Elsie Jane continued with her own desperate campaign of letter-writing and personal contacts, reaching out to anyone who might be able to get her son released. She begged Perley to give Helen the financial split the court had ordered. She promised Perley that he would inherit her farm when she died, adding that she was afraid that without his help to run things there would be nothing left to pass on to him. She pleaded with him to see that he was losing more by being locked up than he could ever hope to gain, but he was too pigheaded to give in. Inasmuch as Elsie Jane had to rely on a horse and buggy to take her the ten miles into town anytime she visited a lawyer, she spent considerable time and much needed energy on her pursuit of Perley's freedom.

Elsie Jane hired what help she could afford. Having a strong work ethic herself, she expected a good day's labor for the low wages she paid. And hired men came and went regularly. One man did work harder and stay longer than the rest, giving Elsie Jane the feeling that this was someone in whom she could place her trust.

John "Mac" MacFarland struck Elsie Jane as an honest, caring man who was willing to work for her in whatever capacity she needed. Gaining her confidence through his work, he also became her advisor, claiming he knew a lawyer by the name of "Mr. Herman" who might be able to help Perley win his freedom. However, this lawyer was expensive and required payment in advance before he would take the case. Desperate for help, Elsie Jane agreed to pay the price. Though Perley had little faith in his fellow man, Elsie Jane had not yet lost hope. In all her seventy-five years she had had very little experience with dishonesty. And if there was any chance that Mac and Mr. Herman could get Perley out of jail, she had to try.

Though it seems hard to believe Elsie would be so gullible, the tales that Mac then fabricated contained enough of a ring of truth to keep her on the hook. He told her that he and Mr. Herman went to the Statehouse in Concord, New Hampshire, to get Perley his pardon but because the members of the "Pardon Board" weren't all at the meeting, they were not able to secure his release. Subsequently, Mac told Elsie that he and the lawyer had traveled to Washington, DC, to secure the pardon. He said that they were there ten days, got the necessary paperwork, but were unable to collect all the required signatures because three of the Board members insisted on being paid $300 each to sign the document. Whether in her innocence or simply wanting so badly for it to be true, Elsie Jane scraped together the money.

Perley

During his absences when Mac was supposedly traveling with lawyer Herman, he was actually at his home a few hours away in Holderness, New Hampshire.

It is hard to imagine that Elsie Jane, if thinking rationally, would have placed that much trust in Mr. MacFarland. But Elsie Jane also felt she was fighting the clock because it was a widely held belief that if someone stayed at the County Farm for more than a year, they would then automatically be transferred to the State Prison in Concord. She was terrified that if Perley was sent to state prison she might never see him again. [Note: This fear on Elsie's part was totally unwarranted. Perley had not been convicted of a criminal offense. Contempt of court was not a crime that would have caused him to be transferred to state prison.]

Once again Mac wrote Elsie Jane and told her he and Mr. Herman had finally gotten the signatures needed for Perley's pardon but on the way home they had a car accident which resulted in both of them being taken to the hospital. He told her he had broken his collarbone and hurt his head and Mr. Herman had a broken hip. Supposedly, they both had spent several weeks in a hospital in Connecticut. Now out of the hospital they would come to see her and arrange for Perley's release just as soon as Mr. Herman could travel. Mac could weave quite an elaborate lie.

A month or two passed before Mac wrote again and told Elsie Jane he and Mr. Herman had attempted to reach her house, getting within two miles when they got mired in the mud so badly they had to turn around. After that Elsie did not hear from Mac again for several months. In despair, she tried writing to Mr. Herman directly. *"I hope it isn't too late to get him* [Perley] *out for I gave most about all my money to pay you to get him home."* Her letter was returned, stamped "unknown." Elsie then wrote to Mac's wife, but received no answer.

ELSIE JANE'S PAIN

Finally, Elsie Jane received a letter from Mac dated June 11, 1935, saying he hadn't been back to see her because he had *"an apsis* [abscess] *in my head and it bursted and my head feels better now."* He went on to say that Mr. Herman had been in the mountains for a month and had been waiting to hear from Mac so they could both drive up, pick up Elsie and get Perley released. With perhaps a touch of conscience after all, Mac signed his letter, *"Give my love to all the family and don't forget your dear Mac. Everything will be alright."*

But Mac's lies were catching up with him. Perley's two half sisters, Myrtie and Festina, had helped their mother raise the money Mac had insisted was necessary for Perley's freedom. Festina's employer became suspicious and trying to look out for her welfare, contacted the local Sheriff to check into the matter. The Sheriff went to MacFarland's house to talk to him but he was not home at the time. After getting a warrant for his arrest, the Sheriff returned to Mac's home the following Sunday, approximately nine months after Mac had started his charade. The Manchester Union newspaper described what happened next: as the Sheriff *"came within sight of the MacFarland house he heard the report of a gun. Going to the living room of the home he found MacFarland lying on the floor, the revolver beside him."* Mrs. MacFarland was still at church, singing in the choir at the time.

A few weeks later, Mrs. MacFarland, who had been unaware of her husband's deception, wrote Elsie a letter apologizing for all Mac had put her through. *"Little did I think,"* she wrote, *"when Mac went to work for you a year ago this is what would happen."* She explained how since his death she had discovered that Mac had a separate post office box where mail from Elsie was delivered; that she knew of no lawyer named Mr. Herman; and as far as she knew Mac had never been hurt or sick a day in his life. It was all lies. *"Why he would do and say the things he did is more than I can tell,"* his widow stated.

In all, "Mac" MacFarland swindled Elsie Jane and other members of the family out of $1,590 promising to secure Perley's release. Ironically, this sum was more than half of what the court had demanded Perley pay Helen in the first place. Perley's pride was costing everyone dearly.

As would be expected, Helen and Elsie Jane were not on the best of terms. Elsie naturally sided with Perley in the dispute and accepted Perley's view of where blame should be placed for the marital breakup. However, it is unlikely Elsie Jane could criticize the job Helen did of caring for her children on her own. She provided them with as stable an upbringing as possible. Money was tight and the children living at home still worked the farm, but Helen tried to give her children what entertainment she could intersperse, often taking them to whist parties held in town, to sugar-on-snow get-togethers with neighbors or having their oldest brother, Harvey, drive the family to Manchester, New Hampshire, in his car to visit their cousins. And the children's schooling continued. Helen wrote to her middle son, Richard, who had joined the Army, of taking little Bernice to a Valentine Party at school where Bernice had received twenty-three valentines, *"more than anyone else."*

Helen seemed to keep a good sense of humor about her predicament, often mentioning the "family politics" in letters, saying, *"maybe my 'conspiracy suit' will be settled and maybe not."* Then she wrote presciently, *"Expect I will die of old age before things are settled."*

Next, due to a bizarre set of events, Elsie Jane found herself before the same judge who had sent Perley to the County Farm. She was arrested for threatening Helen, ostensibly with a gun. From the sketchy account given in the 1936 Manchester Union, Elsie Jane had stopped at Helen's on her way home from town and asked Helen for a chicken which Elsie planned to kill for her Sunday dinner. Helen obliged and fetched the chicken. Elsie Jane then complained that it was too small and allegedly drew a revolver and wielded it in a threatening manner. Helen called the Sheriff, who immediately went to Elsie Jane's house but could find no revolver. Nevertheless, Elsie Jane was taken to the city of Keene to appear before the judge. She pleaded not guilty, told the court that she never owned a revolver and denied making any threat. Whether due to her lack of credibility or because of her relationship with Perley...or the judge felt he needed no further evidence to convict her, Elsie Jane was found guilty and was ordered to furnish a bond in the sum of $200 to keep the peace for a year.

It is hard to imagine that Elsie Jane at age seventy-six would pull a gun on Helen. But in a letter to Perley a few months later his oldest sister, Festina, implied that it might have, in fact, happened. She wrote that if her mother hadn't been so overwrought with worry, she *"would never have gone over to Helen's that time and acted the way she did."*

For obvious reasons, Perley's siblings were becoming more and more upset over the effects his incarceration was having on their mother. As in most family dramas, it is not just the main participants who are affected. All too often a family conflict can have a devastating impact on a much wider circle of friends and relatives. Perley, in his single-minded determination to redeem his honor, gave very little thought to how his actions were affecting those who cared most for him.

Newspaper headlines - June 1935
Reprinted with permission from The Manchester Union

Elsie Jane Swett around 1935

Chapter Twelve
Time to Go

It was becoming quite obvious to everyone at the County Farm that Perley had to go. The Superintendent and staff were sick of his contentiousness and the judge who sent him there had never expected him to hold out so long in his refusal to give in to the demands of the court. Perley's incarceration now had lasted over three years, longer than any other sentence served by an inmate at the Westmoreland County Farm, past or present. And Perley was still willing to stubbornly spend the rest of his life in jail rather than give Helen her due.

Everyone involved in his case was anxious to find a solution but until Perley complied with the court's order he was still "in contempt" and could not simply be allowed to go free. A "high county official" even ordered medical tests to determine Perley's mental competency, hoping he could be found legally insane so they would have the excuse to send him to an asylum. Instead, Perley passed with flying colors.

It seemed Perley was the only one who was not trying desperately to win his freedom. *"I have no wish to leave jail to become a pauper,"* Perley said. Furthermore, he repeatedly wrote to his mother that he would never return to his old neighborhood without an apology from his ex-wife and oldest son, who Perley felt had aided Helen in sending him to jail. Without that apology and restoration of his *"good name and reputation,"* Perley had no desire to go back into society. Refusing to accept the court's terms and knowing how anxious the people who sent him to jail now were to get rid of him, Perley felt he had regained a slight degree of control over his life. Freedom would only be accepted on *his* terms, which now included being compensated for *"damages as well as justice."* Perley still hoped to find a *"good and honest"* lawyer who would help him recover financial damages for his suffering, which he now assigned a value of $15,000.

There is no telling how long the impasse would have gone on if Helen herself hadn't made the ultimate concession to allow Perley his freedom: she died.

During those last few stressful years, Helen's health had deteriorated. She often felt too tired to keep up with the daily chores. In May, 1937, she was admitted to the local hospital to have her gallbladder removed. She survived the operation but internal bleeding took her life a few days later. She was only forty-nine years old, the exact same age to the day as Perley. Helen was buried in the Sullivan cemetery next to her child who had died so young and under mysterious circumstances. Perley was not allowed to attend her funeral. Their children, aged nine to twenty-five, were now motherless and virtually fatherless.

Everyone felt Perley should be home now to take care of his family. But, even with Helen's death, Perley wasn't immediately released. It finally took a heart-wrenching letter from his mother to Judge James to give the court system the excuse it was looking for:

"Kind Judge,

I will write a few lines to you about my son, Perley E. Swett. He has been in jail in Westmoreland three years. I need him so much, he was always so good to help me. Haying is coming soon and I can't do that. And no money to hire it done. I am a poor, uneducated old woman. I don't know much about the law, but I do know I want and need Perley here. I was 78 the 7th of last Jan., 1937. If I live to be 100 I never will have so many 7s again. I am too old to have the care of the farm. You sent Perley to jail, now please, Dear Judge, won't you get him out or tell me how I can do it? The last time I went to see him, that isn't very often for it is a long, hard ride for me, he said he had been in there 1000 & 5 days. He don't count the weeks or months, but the days, poor boy. I hope to hear from you soon and have my dear boy back here with me to help me. I need him so much. Very respectfully yours, Elsie J. Swett"

In discussing the matter, the lawyers and judge decided this could, finally, be their way to get Perley out of the House of Corrections and still save face. With Helen's death, they could treat Elsie Jane's letter as a petition to the court for Perley's release. The clerk of court suggested, however, that the *"petition should come from Perley as he is the one that should "bend the neck."* Judge James agreed and the necessary forms were sent to Perley for his signature. The matter would finally be over and Perley would be a free man. As the Superior Court Clerk said in his letter to the Judge, *"this man has been in too long and it seems to me it might be a good idea to get rid of him without further fuss. It is just about the same kind of a proposition as getting a bull by the tail."*

The petition was promptly mailed to Elsie Jane who was instructed to send it to Perley, have him sign it and then it could be brought before the Judge. Elsie Jane was weak with relief and did as she was told; to her dismay Perley refused to sign. In explanation, he wrote his mother:

"I did not sign that paper for it was made out in a way that sounded like I would be signing the death warrant to my plans and hopes. I am trying to get justice and think more of

that than I do of getting out of jail. You may forget I have a nine year old girl to fight for and the means to support her, it will take several thousand dollars to pay damage to my health that will reduce my future earning power below what it used to be. The county should and I believe can be held responsible for that. As well as for being improperly and unlawfully put and kept in jail. The least that I ever could consider as a settlement would be a full reinstatement of damage caused me and an acknowledgment of injustice in a satisfactory way to me."

Now what to do! In another letter to the Judge, the County Solicitor wrote:

"Dear Judge James:
In the famous Perley Swett matter all of the attorneys who represented Mr. Swett and were unsuccessful in their efforts to secure his release, have now dropped by the wayside. In accordance with your suggestions to Judge Madden I drew a petition simply stating the situation in a few words and asking for the release of Mr. Swett. I sent it to Mr. Swett through his mother. He now refuses to sign this petition.
As County Solicitor I have been besieged by the keeper of the House of Correction to get him out of there if I possibly could on the grounds that he is rather difficult to handle and is not much use to them. Is there any way in which this matter could be brought before you for action without Perley signing the petition?"

Only then did the Judge decide that this was the only course of action. Elsie Jane's letter was returned to him by the court clerk and accepted, without signature, as basis for Perley's release:

Perley

"*Dear Judge James:*

Enclosed find letter of Mrs. Swett, which I understand you are going to treat as a petition. I think that while Perley kicks about the House of Correction, really he will miss it when he is tossed out into the cold world, but most of us agree that something must be done to get rid of him. Charles Madden, clerk of court."

The Judge's response was, "*I think this order will be more punishment than the order of May, 1934.*" Finally, on August 7, 1937, through none of his own doing, Perley was released from the House of Correction. Like it or not, Perley was now a free man.

As Perley feared, though, he did not have much to look forward to. His ex-wife was dead, his children were mostly grown and embarked on lives of their own, and most were estranged from him. All of his money was gone. Because he was still legally required to give Helen's estate (and its beneficiaries, his own children) the financial split decreed by the court in their divorce, Perley would soon find himself in a battle with his oldest son. And although the country was just coming out of a depression, there were not a lot of opportunities for a tired and discouraged fifty year old man to rebuild his fortune, let alone even find work. Freedom did not offer much promise on that warm summer day when Perley was finally sent home.

Throughout the rest of his life Perley would often recall those three years he spent locked up. "*I think I have dreamed at least a hundred times of being back there and of being threatened and abused.*"

Perley Edwin Swett

Chapter Thirteen
"I Have Never Found a Companion So Companionable as Solitude"
Henry David Thoreau

Perley had sworn that without an apology from his family for the role he believed they had in sending him to jail, he would never return to live in his old neighborhood. But without money or job he did not have a choice. So he returned to the old farmhouse where he and Helen had loved and quarreled and raised their children for almost twenty years. Though he had fought so hard to hold onto it, he would never be totally comfortable in his home again.

By now his children had all moved away and the large house, much like his life, was empty. With no transportation it would be difficult for him to visit his family. Furthermore, his affection for them had always seemed contingent on how high they placed him on a pedestal. And in their eyes that pedestal had long ago slipped out from under Perley. Some of the children blamed him for their mother's death. The youngest daughter was only four when Perley left home. Now she was nine and lived with her oldest brother, Harvey, and his new wife. They were her legal guardians.

Harvey could not forgive the way his father had treated his mother. Entering his twenties when his father first moved out, it had fallen to Harvey to step in to fill his father's vacant shoes and help care for his younger siblings.

Now, as administrator of Helen's estate and representing the interests of the other children, Harvey started proceedings to force Perley to give up the assets originally mandated by the court as soon as he learned that his father was to be discharged from jail. Within two weeks of his release, Perley was served with court papers which continued the fight. Everything that Perley or Elsie Jane owned had an attachment placed on it by Helen's estate.

For another year, Perley fought to keep his property (which had miraculously found its way back into Perley's possession after being in his mother's name). In the end, he finally relented. Perley gave three tracts of land totaling over 300 acres to Helen's estate to be divided among his children as their inheritance. Perley was allowed to keep his "home place" (where he continued to live alone) and several other tracts of land as his share.

Naturally, the property settlement didn't sit well with Perley and for almost thirty years it caused him to be estranged from his eldest son, Harvey. Until the day he died, Perley never quite forgave his children for forcing him into giving up his land. Though resentments eased with time, Perley intended that his children would never inherit any more of his property.

With Helen's estate finally settled in March, 1939, Perley turned his energies and attention back to recouping some of the losses he felt he had suffered by being held at the County Farm. Perley's goal was to sue the County for $15,000 for *"over three years illegal and unlawful confinement and abuse in jail causing a heavy financial loss as well as serious damage to the health of the complainant."* As a consequence, *"A satisfactory settlement and financial remuneration is demanded."* Once again he wrote lawyer after lawyer looking for someone to represent him. And once again, each declined his urgent plea.

Over time Perley finally accepted that there was no hope of being awarded damages and reluctantly gave up the quest. Resigned to final defeat, Perley kept to himself for the next few years. This time his solitary confinement was self-imposed.

Perley had very few friends or allies left. His own brother had committed treason when he testified for Helen's defense at the divorce trial. Even a trip into town was painful for Perley because of what he imagined his neighbors were saying behind his back. Only in Elsie Jane's dependence and motherly affection did Perley find solace.

During this time of Perley's seclusion, an old friend and former neighbor finally made her way back to the area. For ten years Florence Brooks-Aten had shuttled between friends and relatives, mostly in the New York area, staying with whoever would shelter her and had an empty bed. For a while she lived in a small, one room upstairs apartment in Newark, New Jersey, and worked on a turkey farm. But the foul air aggravated her 'bronchial condition'. Her doctor suggested Florence move back to New Hampshire.

An elderly aunt purchased a small cottage for Florence on Wilson Pond in the town of Swanzey, about twenty miles from Shinbone Shack and her former estate. Of her new home she wrote to Elsie Jane: *"They gave me all the comforts anyone would wish for. A nice stove (enamel), Frigidaire, new sink and bathtub installed, coal and wood and a 1938 Chevrolet Coupe. I had been without for so long that I can hardly believe it is true. With what my sister and aunt and cousins give me each month I can, with economy, pay the few running expenses."* Florence was then sixty-four years old.

She went on to reminisce in her letter that she missed spending Thanksgiving dinners with the Swett family. *"I wish*

I could have come to Thanksgiving as it was the first one I've been alone and didn't have a dinner. Sat at home and kept warm, did a little mending and listened to my radio." She wanted to visit but with the war starting *"the gas rationing and tires do not warrant my using my car for any trips and as the road to your place is so stony and hard on tires I haven't tried to go up, but have wanted to so much. Never a day goes by that I do not dream I am home in my shack and listening to the wind in the spruces and hear the birds and listen to the water rush over the dam and dream of living in the lovely house for which I have had so many plans to live."* Perhaps it was easier to live with her memories than it would have been to revisit all that she had lost.

Possibly another reason Florence never made it back to visit Perley's family was because she was such a poor driver. A friend of the motor vehicle inspector who gave Florence her driving test at that time recounted the story he had told her: *"Florence Brooks Aten was such a horrible driver that after failing the driving test four times he [*the instructor*] felt sorry for her and gave her a license with the strict understanding that she never drive on the main streets of the city of Keene."* Probably the inspector did not want her returning for a fifth try. During her last driving test, when the car was heading toward the bushes, he had to reach over her lap to grab the emergency brake. In doing so, his watch caught on her stockings. She then adamantly insisted he buy her a new pair.

Florence never did see the completion of her lodge. For many years it stood as a shell, inviting destruction by vandals and the elements. Like Perley, she felt victimized by others, never accepting responsibility for her misfortunes. And despite being surrounded by neighbors on Wilson Pond, she became almost as reclusive.

Perley

With the United States entry into World War II, many manufacturing jobs became available in New Hampshire. Many of Perley's neighbors had grown disenchanted with the constant drudgery of farming. Instead, they decided to move closer to the factories in the cities for shorter hours and steady wages. The once active neighborhood that Perley had grown up in was becoming more and more deserted.

Though Perley fought against it, the Town of Stoddard decided to discontinue maintaining the road to Elsie's farm. In reality, very few repairs had been made on the road for the last twenty years anyway. With no close neighbors and hardly any traffic, Perley and his mother rarely saw another human being. *"Very seldom these two miles are repaired or winter snows plowed,"* Perley wrote, *"and no one seems to care."*

Sadly, Perley continued to be estranged from his children who were starting families of their own. By now, his first grandchild had entered the world, the daughter of his oldest son, Harvey. But this grandchild, and her siblings to follow, would not meet their grandfather until they had grown into their teens. Perley's twin daughters, Dorothy and Dora, whom he had so cherished when they were young, were now married and having children. Yet he rarely saw them. (*"Twins I had to love for a few years, while young...and then lost after they were grown and married."*) Perley's other two sons, Richard and Maurice, had gone to serve in World War II. Though he wrote numerous letters of complaint to lawyers and local newspapers, Perley never wrote to his sons.

The rest of the country was plunged into war, faced daily with rationing, black-out drills and fear that loved ones would never return home. But Perley and his mother remained insulated, their lives focused on self-sufficiency, virtually untouched by the war. Their seclusion, however, would not keep death from their door.

Perley's favorite sister, Nora, lived twenty miles away in the city of Keene with her husband, Charles Partridge. Nora was a beautiful woman who, much like Perley, always spoke her mind. She did not always tell Perley what he wanted to hear, but he did respect her honesty and appreciated her desire to remain in regular contact with both he and their mother, Elsie Jane.

Nora suffered from migraines. One day at the end of November, 1943, after putting supper on the table for her husband, she felt a headache coming on and decided to go for a walk in the cool evening air. Nora was never seen alive again. Friends, neighbors and police searched for Nora, with no luck. Once more, Elsie Jane was forced to relive her childhood nightmare of waiting despairingly for news when her own father went missing. Finally, on April 1st of the following year, three months after she disappeared, two young boys playing by the water's edge found Nora's body floating in the Ashuelot River not far from her home. No foul play was ever suspected and her death was ruled an accident. Likely she simply fell into the river and drowned as she, like all of the Swett children, had never learned to swim. Nora was fifty-seven when she died, just one year younger than her grandfather, Jonathan Whittier, when he "died by the wayside" in a snowstorm.

Nora's death hit Elsie Jane particularly hard. A strong will and body had carried her through many adversities in her long life but losing her daughter this way seemed to break her spirit. Life was running out of her and her health began to deteriorate. It became obvious to everyone - including Perley who had been caring for her from his neighboring homestead - that she could no longer live alone. And Perley finally did what he had to, moving back to his birthplace to provide comfort and care to a loving mother who had always done the same for him.

Perley

On January 7, 1944, Elsie Jane turned eighty-five; it would be her last year. She had reached the age she always said she would. It had been twenty-one years since her husband, Daniel, died. Elsie had predicted she would continue to live the twenty-one year age difference between them...and she did.

Elsie Jane had made it known to her family that she wanted to die in her own home as her husband had done. When it was obvious the end was near, Perley still gave his mother the option of going to the hospital but she chose to stay in her beloved home with her favorite son. She could not think of a better way to face the end. Perley honored her wishes and made her as comfortable as he could.

In the book, "More Spit than Polish," (published in 1987 by Yankee Publishing Incorporated of Dublin, NH) F.B.Tolman, author and distant neighbor, wrote an account of visiting the Swetts while looking for her lost dog. Elsie Jane was on her death bed at that time:

"The Swetts lived at the remote end of nowhere. At one time, many years before, that road had connected two small towns, but all the residents that lived along it except the Swetts had moved away, and the road had been "thrown up." In the best of times it hadn't been much; now it was just two ruts wandering through the woods, mulching its way past cellar holes, past the crumbling remains of a sheep barn, around boulders, down ledges. A road made by wagon wheels and suitable only for wagon wheels.

The Swetts' house was weathered grey, the clapboards curled and brittle, the grooves in the front door deeply channeled. Supporting the house on one side was a shed containing a tangle of old boards, old wheels, old machinery, and a white bathtub to water the goats.

> *Perley himself was dapper in overalls, a red handkerchief round his neck, and his white hair aflourish on the sides of his brown, bald skull.*
>
> *Perley explained that he'd been slow to get the word out (that he found the dog) because his mother had been poorly and he didn't like to leave her. In fact, she'd been in bed for days, just lay there-hadn't seen anybody-she just lay there-he wondered whether it might do her good to see someone, might stir her up some. Maybe I would stop in a minute?*
>
> *She was in one of the two front rooms; it had probably been the parlor. (The other must have been the kitchen, but the glimpse I got revealed nothing but tables piled up with cans, newspapers, bottles, and more and more papers.) Mrs. Swett was lying on a bed so low it seemed only a foot off the floor. Later I realized that this must have been because there were no bedsprings; the mattress was laid across ropes strung on the frame. An old hound dog dozed at the foot and raised his head briefly as I entered. A table beside the bed held an assortment of patent medicines and a jelly glass with wilted daisies. The rest of the room was crowded with bulging burlap sacks. What could they have held? Perley was obviously afflicted with pack-rat-itis.*
>
> *It may have been her features or perhaps her expression that made her seem so beautiful - whatever it was, she had a kind of beauty as natural as a shaft of light. Her face was delicate, fine-boned, her skin hazel brown, her hair fresh and white. Something about her made me think of an idealized portrait of an American Indian, her eyes were so dark, so self-contained and peaceful. It was the face of one who was waiting, without fear."*

Elsie Jane passed away quietly on August 18, 1944 from bronchial pneumonia. Her family missed her greatly. Perley composed the epitaph for her gravestone:

Perley

Memories will for years remain behind,
 though she may sleep far away;
Her heart and farm were so entwined,
 she seldom leave it even for a day;
In the Whittier lot close by this home so dear,
 a place for her did wait;
But she chose her last sleep to be near,
 Elsie Jane Shannon, [her mother-in-law]
 and her mate.

Daniel and Elsie Jane Swett
Taken around 1912

Chapter Fourteen
"Housekeeper Wanted"

To care for his mother, Perley had, of necessity, returned to the home where he was born. Now that Elsie Jane was gone, Perley was free to move back to his own homestead or to make a totally new start someplace else. But what had he to gain from a new start? The "outside" world held little promise to Perley. It was a hostile world that, over time, had tried its best to strip him of his possessions and his pride. Although only fifty-six years old, the lessons of those years weighed heavily on Perley. His wife and family, his mother and his money were gone. But he still owned some land...and land offered comfort, security and the means to sustain himself. Better to hold on to what he had left and continue in the security of the life he knew.

Perhaps Perley was thinking of Florence Aten and how quickly she lost everything when he wrote the following to his younger sister, Ella: *"Got a ton of potatoes delivered for twenty dollars, so have shelter, warmth and food. And I do not have to worry about losing my job in case of hard times or being evicted as long as I can keep taxes paid. It would take more than the lure of comforts and luxuries of city life to offset the feeling of safety and security that I seem to posses here, where emigration has left me a 'hermit'."*

He further explained his reasoning, *"You may ask why I don't move to a village or city. But I like the woods on the old home farm and wish to continue living here. Also, I can very nearly, though not quite, forget the crookedness and corruption of officials and others that have been to blame for my being looked upon even by many of my former townspeople as almost an outcast in society."* These same sentiments were captured in his poetry as well:

> *"By trusting others and their promises too often*
> *he believed,*
> *Some solace were found here and less chance*
> *to be deceived;*
> *Crowded streets and steady noise he never could endure,*
> *No costly foods and rents for him, as cities*
> *held no allure."*

Though never having recovered his full strength and vitality after his years in jail, Perley still attempted to make some repairs to the old farm. But he did not have the resources or energy to tackle all the work needed to refurbish the family home after one hundred years of neglect. In addition, with the road no longer maintained in either direction and it being prohibitively expensive to string electric lines over two miles for one person, Perley had little choice but to continue to live in the same primitive manner as his parents and grandparents.

Henry David Thoreau wrote, *"Live free and uncommitted. It makes but little difference whether you are committed to a farm or the county jail."* It is unlikely Perley would have agreed with that sentiment, having experienced both situations. Being imprisoned and subject to the rules and whims of his jailers was hardly the same as being committed to survival on a farm that had been in his family for generations. And it is certain that Thoreau had many more friends and supporters than Perley did. *"Just 30 days since anyone been here, so* only about a week since have been out of bread, but have plenty of crackers and canned goods."

Perley's only contact with family was through letters and it was an eleven mile round-trip tramp to get his mail. Local hunters knew Perley's predicament and would stop for his mail which was being held for him at Jack's country store in Sullivan. *"Got mail from November the first day of April. See no one in March, a trapper once in February and road agent and his helper last day of January. A loaf of bread my sister sent up then were only fresh groceries got the first three months this year."*

Through all his real and imagined hardships, Perley still retained his quirky sense of humor. He wrote in reply to a cousin who had tried to persuade Perley to abandon the farm and move into town: *"Sorry I can't take your advice and 'sell out', but prefer living on the old home farm, even though winters are long and cold. But like the quiet and do not expect to starve or freeze to death. Also, very little danger of being run over by traffic."*

Perley's one lifeline to civilization and the only "modern" convenience was a telephone. He seemed to think it might come in handy one day, *"in case of sickness or death, so to send for the undertaker."*

Perley would boast that it was the oldest connection in town, having been hooked up for his parents back in 1907. The original phone was still in use at that time, a *"hand-crank style that was placed on a wall post in the kitchen nearly fifty years ago."* The phone was actually little more than a decoration all those years, as it seldom worked. When it did, the static was so bad it was almost impossible to hear what was being said.

Because there were not enough people living nearby to warrant putting up telephone poles, the phone wires were tacked to trees, sometimes no more than a foot or two off the ground. Perley described the condition of the system: *"Part of the wire has never been replaced except by patching broken places. About one mile goes through the woods and in several places tree growth had totally enclosed one or both wires."* Once or twice a month, Perley had to hook the lines back up after they were knocked down during a storm. If there was a heavy rain, phone service could be lost for days or more until the wires dried out.

Perley complained in writing to the phone company whenever his service was disrupted for more than a few days. When his phone was out of commission for five weeks after a severe storm, the company appeased him by taking a few cents off his monthly bill. And although Perley was unhappy about the size of his telephone bills (*"When put in here I believe the monthly cost of the phone was one dollar and a half. Now it is a little over four (including tax),"* he promptly paid them. He imagined that the officials at the phone company were looking for any excuse to disconnect his line as the upkeep on it each month surely cost more than Perley paid.

Ever willing to sport with anyone that might attempt to take advantage of him, Perley sent this poem to the president of the local phone company, showing he fully recognized the company's plight:

In due time your report of service failure to my desk and attention came,
You will get a proper rebate soon given, as we cannot dispute your claim;
We always try to give the best of service, regardless of our income or expense,
And we raise the rates only in odd years, and then by just a few cents.

Perley

*Of course we lose some of our poorer customers, and wish
you would also fail to pay,
So we could have a valid excuse to discard your line and take
your phone away;
The most expensive branch line this company ever has seen,
and even worse has lately grown,
Nearly four miles of wires over a dead end road for your
benefit alone.*

Before the 'dial-up' system went into effect, there could be as many as eight to ten parties on each of the approximately twenty lines in Sullivan. Everyone had their own sequence of rings to know when the call was for them. Perley's "number" was "Line 5, Ring 2." If someone wanted to call him they would first crank the handle on the phone which then sent an electric charge over the wire to signal the operator. She would connect the caller to Perley's line and press two short rings to alert all the people on Line 5 that this call was for Perley. Though he lived in Stoddard, Perley's phone service originated from the town of Sullivan.

The Hastings family of East Sullivan was in charge of the town's phone system for almost twenty years. Brenda Hastings Parker spent many hours helping her mother and grandmother take care of the switchboard in their home. She reminisced about one of the perks of having party lines. *"If neighbors decided they wanted to listen in, all they had to do was quietly pick up the phone when it rang. Each added listener diminished the strength of the signal which made it very difficult for anyone to hear what was being said, but it was a good way for neighbors to keep up with the local gossip. It was not uncommon to hear several clicks when you answered your phone to indicate there were people listening to your conversation."*

Brenda remembered the day in 1956 when the telephone man came to their house to "cut the cable." This was when all the phones in town went to the dial-up system, eliminating the need for an operator. Perley, like many townspeople, had been upset with this technological advance and, of course, had already written a letter of complaint. *"I believe a large majority of phone users would vote against a 'dial' system to take the place of the system now in effect."* Brenda remembered people calling in panic, worried that without an operator's help, they would no longer be able to reach someone in an emergency. It would take a while for them to understand that they could now place their calls direct.

Having made the decision to live at his birthplace, Perley rented out his former homestead for $4.00 a week. Despite this paltry amount, his tenants fell behind in their payments. After trying unsuccessfully to collect the money due him, Perley once again resorted to legal action. And once again, the legal system let him down. In a poem titled "Troubles of a Small Country Landlord," he penned:

Lawyers tell me I cannot collect, and so from both must lose,
Besides the cost of eviction, if to leave the tenants may not choose;
On the fat of the land they can live with their rent unpaid,
Yet there is no law that will give a poor landlord aid.

This time Perley would reach out to higher authority. He wrote to President Truman to complain that New Hampshire law did nothing to protect the landlord. Not surprisingly, his protests brought no satisfaction. And his trust of the justice system and of those who practiced law diminished further.

In 1947 Perley bought his first goats with the intention of raising them for meat, milk and to sell. The herd grew quickly and before long it required a significant investment of time and energy. His new side venture was becoming a full time job. *"Had ten baby goats born on the same day. Was almost on twenty-four hour nursing duty for a few days."*

Perley, like his mother, had a deep fondness for all animals. His goats were now the sole beneficiaries of Perley's attentions. As his herd grew, Perley found himself acting as nurse, midwife, and surrogate mother. One goat, that had dragged itself home on it's knees after being crippled in a trap set by hunters, was allowed to stay in the warmth and comfort of the house at night where Perley cared for it. As the goat's legs healed it was able to spend days outside with the rest of the herd. But when this crippled goat became pregnant, Perley allowed it to give birth and raise the baby in his house. The baby goat seemed to think Perley was its mother as it would often leave the flock during the day to follow Perley around as he did his chores.

Within a few years, Perley's goats numbered over one hundred. Seldom were they sold anymore and then only with the strict instructions that they were to be raised as pets, not for meat. For Perley had formed a connection again. Though it was not a human bond, Perley felt some security in knowing that his goats would never leave him. He was their lord and master. And they were more than pets. They were good company in the lonely Stoddard hills.

On Christmas Eve, 1952, Perley witnessed what he took to be a miraculous birth. One of his goats delivered triplets. He was struck not just by this occurrence but by its timing which he took as a prophetic sign to be shared. Young C. Arthur Bradley had just graduated from seminary in New York City. Though used to city life, his first assignment was to serve a parish of three small churches in three adjacent towns in southern New Hampshire. On that same Christmas Eve of his first year as minister, Reverend Bradley had returned from an early church service for the children of the town of Gilsum. He had just settled down by himself to listen to Danny Kaye's 'Hans Christian Anderson' and fight off a bout of homesickness when the phone rang.

"*This is Perley Swett.*" The connection crackled. "*We've just had triplets born up here.*" At first Reverend Bradley thought surely the neighborhood teenagers were playing a joke on him. Then he remembered meeting Perley when he had made his rounds to meet all his new parishioners. Though he recalled they had a nice visit, Perley showed no interest in attending church.

"*Yes,*" Perley continued. "*We've had triplets here and they are just beautiful. I was hoping you could come up to see them.*" Triplets? Born on that isolated farm way up in the woods? Curious but still wondering if Perley was pulling his leg, Reverend Bradley nevertheless "*went along with the gag.*"

As the Reverend remembered the incident over fifty years later, he looked back upon that Christmas Eve as one of the most memorable of his life. "*In talking with Perley, I realized he was lonely and overwhelmed with the birth of triplet goats on Christmas Eve and he wanted to share the good news.*" Reverend Bradley further recalled, "*I must say it made my night. That this old hermit of Sullivan was open to the wonder of the miracle of birth, even of three baby goats, on the anniversary of the birth of the Christ child. It made me appreciate Christmas in a way I had never done before.*"

At the end of their conversation Reverend Bradley told Perley that "*as soon as mud season is over this spring I will come up to see them.*" True to his word, the Reverend made the difficult journey up to Perley's when spring came although history does not record if any out of the ordinary baptisms took place!

Though the goats were a comfort to Perley, he still missed human contact. While he had no desire to move away from his home, Perley never really enjoyed being totally isolated. *"Being alone is not my idea of Heaven,"* he wrote, *"but it is better than those previous twenty-five years"* [of his marriage].

When the loneliness weighed too heavily on him and no longer owning a horse, Perley would walk the five to six miles into town to attend card parties held at the town hall. This was something he had enjoyed doing before his incarceration. As old resentments lessened, Perley actually began to enjoy visiting in town, though the distance and difficulty of getting there kept such visits to a minimum.

With the roads to his farm all but impassable, Perley had few visitors. But those who happened by (hunters or disoriented travelers) were generally friendly. Occasionally someone with a 4-wheel drive offered to take Perley into the city of Keene to replenish his supplies. As time passed, Perley was discovering that people in the "outside world" - and even in his own family - were not as critical of him as he once believed they would be. To be sure, he had found protection from adversaries by his withdrawal from society. But he was also finding that living a life of mere subsistence engendered in others the desire to offer comfort and aid if only he'd accept it. Perhaps he just needed to reach out more to others. So slowly, Perley was coming out of his cocoon, opening himself up to the possibility that a better life could be had. Perhaps a life with a new partner.

Perley had always faced life's challenges in his own unique fashion, half as a realist and half as a romantic dreamer. On one hand he reasoned that he needed help running the farm, especially as he grew older. On the other hand he fantasized that there might be a woman "out there" who would fill that role and also provide the warmth and affection missing in his life. He recalled that widowers of earlier generations often advertised for young housekeepers who eventually married their employers. Indeed, Perley had seen this happen in Helen's own family where circumstances were far from ideal. After Helen's father had shot himself in 1912, he hired several housekeepers to care for him...and eventually married one who was only twenty-one.

Now Perley had a mission. But after many years spent in a failed marriage, this time he'd get it right. And that meant leaving nothing to chance. First, he had to make the terms of his proposal crystal clear so the "right" woman could not possibly misunderstand what he was looking for. Second, he had to get the word out as broadly as possible. His means of doing this was a poem entitled "Housekeeper Wanted." Perley had five hundred copies printed which he made sure were passed out all over town.

Housekeeper Wanted
(on J. Whittier farm)

A brown haired girl, very honest, pleasing and calm,
 And well under the legal voting age of today;
But that on a rocky and very isolated farm,
 May care all the rest of her life to stay.

English stock preferred, and standard quality far above,
 Or any ordinary "run of the mills,"
Quiet and brave instead of bold, very faithful in love,
 And willing to live among these lonely granite hills.

Neat and healthy, more than husky built, or fast,
 But ready to help on any kind of work, or chores;
For the farm owner's youth is long since past,
 And much of her labor might need to be outdoors.

Perley

Plenty of work needing always to be done,
 In the forlorn house, and barn, and all;
With seldom any chance for movies, or fun,
 And no near neighbors on which to call.

Modern conveniences on this farm in Stoddard South-West
 May never expect or hope to be found;
This dead end highway very often a severe test,
 For a F.W.D., with the driver sober and sound.

House and barn old, and like the owner, very staid,
 And only a few acres of tillable land still clear;
Can any very young, and poor, but qualifying maid,
 Want to live the rest of her lifetime here?

Smoking is banned, and also beer,
 But she need not be a picture star;
Good eyes, but that may see few relatives appear,
 Back in the woods so far,
Yet must of wild land be fond,
 and for lonely solitude to care;
For in the region of Taylor pond,
 any passing traffic is in the air.

Only a super-perfect girl may be hired,
 Ready for a farm life extra hard;
Doubtless some orphan is desired,
 But others will not be barred.

If fully qualifying, and it plainly shows,
 Willing to learn and no shirk;
So useless verse the owner may compose,
 While she does all the needed work.

"Housekeeper Wanted"

Very few all the qualifications perhaps may fill,
And have eyes and hair dark, but softly brown;
Just a little scarce but must be in existence still,
And doubtless more than one in New York town.

But these earthly angels are not very easily discovered,
Though many might be living between Oregon and Maine;
Yet unless the abode of one may be soon uncovered,
Perhaps this old farm-house may never have a "house-keeper" again.
     By Pearl Whittier (Perley Swett)

  Aware or not of the snickers and gossip his poem was generating, Perley attempted to have it published in the local newspaper. The editor promptly refused, stating, "In reading your copy, we feel that a respondent would believe there was matrimonial intent." But the poem was having an effect, bringing a great deal of notoriety to the Hermit of Taylor Pond and, remarkably, even some applicants. To Perley's chagrin, however, they were not young women who might be willing to settle down with him on his secluded farm and bear him more children. Instead applicants tended to be more mature women. One wrote to Perley asking why he wouldn't consider someone over fifty. *"I believe it would be beyond your ability,"* he answered, *"to lead the horse to plow and to be carrying a baby in your spare arm."*

  Perley was willing to lower the bar when it came to a candidate's appearance, however. Explaining that though he was willing to forego a *"magazine cover girl,"* he would still like someone that was *"not too bad to look at across a four foot table and with a weight not to exceed my own, around 130 now."*

One could easily view "Housekeeper Wanted" as the fantasy of a mind set to wander by too many years of solitary confinement. Nothing could be farther from the truth. For Perley possessed the intelligence and the wit to fully grasp the irony of his own writing...as well as the public response it would provoke. Yes, his poem embraced his complete wish list (why aim lower?) in the remote possibility that some young woman might actually be willing to buy what he had to sell. But "Housekeeper Wanted" was also a canny "send-up," the way to bring him the attention he wanted. For Perley was discovering that his own reclusiveness could be turned to advantage, attracting the curiosity and interest of others. This would be his passport out of solitary confinement.

Indeed, his poem had already started enjoyable correspondence with a number of women, mitigating the fact that *"a hermit's pen-pals are most as scarce as hen's teeth."* And by keeping his standards ridiculously high, he built in the protection he needed for never finding exactly the right candidate.

> *"Just a small backwoods farmer, and I now live all alone,*
> *Though to get a housekeeper I have several times tried;*
> *Doubtless I am too exacting, I will this freely own,*
> *Yet very few girls to choose from have ever applied."*

Perley continued to send ads for 'housekeepers' to the local newspapers. When they produced no results he tried branching out to newspapers in Manchester and Boston. He also wrote to different organizations such as the Salvation Army, religious groups, the YWCA, even to the Chief of Police. Nothing produced his "perfect mate" even though he offered a one hundred dollar reward for help in securing her. *"It seems as if any girl I would want,"* he complained, *"I*

can't get and the ones I might be able to get, I do not want!"
But Perley knew how to get attention.

In the coming years Perley, a twinkle in his eye, often joked and flirted with women of all ages who wrote to him or visited. Still handing out his poem, its humor was now out in the open. For it is likely that Perley was never more than half serious in his quest for a young housekeeper/wife. *"Someone told me if I ever married a teenage girl I ought to have my head examined."* He explained realistically in a letter, *"I disagreed with them as I believe she would be the one to need the head examination, instead of me!"*

If a woman actually showed an interest, Perley always found an excuse why she did not meet his "ideal." It seems likely he would have sabotaged any relationship that showed promise. And we finally understand why in a poem Perley wrote much later on:

Our wedding date always brings remembrance of a little happiness known,
When you were once to me a wife and willing by my side to sleep,
I wanted kisses and your arms around me, yet I was made to sleep alone,
Remembrances of those bygone years are all that are left for me to keep.

Our birthday makes me think of those years so long gone by,
I have tried so hard to forget you, an impossibility so it seems,
A man may die with a broken heart, too proud to be seen to cry,
But a man can never forget the girl who holds first place in his dreams.

Perley attempting to repair the roof on the attached shed which served as the entryway to his house

Perley with his goats

Chapter Fifteen
Frugality Rules

In between Perley's romantic daydreams, there was always work to be done to help take his mind off his loneliness. But with only himself to please, Perley settled into the routine of doing only what was necessary for his daily survival and reasonable comfort. That gave him time to write poetry and letters, and care for the goats. His hours each day were filled.

Perley continued to invest the money he could scrape together in small tracts of land in Stoddard and the surrounding towns. The majority of his income came from selling trees off his home farm to logging companies. This enabled him to buy more parcels of land, whereupon he repeated the process of "logging off" the available hardwoods and pine before reselling the land at a profit.

At times Perley cut and split firewood himself which he sold by the cord to anyone who was able to drive in to pick it up. In 1951 he was selling a cord of wood for one dollar. Within five years his price had risen to seven dollars a cord.

Perley also cut and sold spruce and balsam Christmas trees for ten to thirty cents each. *"Would be a rich man if I could get 30c a piece for every spruce or balsam tree on my land."*

Perley was tenacious about ferreting out land deals that might turn a profit for him. Unable to locate T. Leonard

MacBean who had purchased Florence Aten's former estate, and having been told that he was an elusive character who kept well out of the public eye, Perley wrote to MacBean's daughter, *"I do not know if your father may be in the approximate class with Columbus, William Tell, Diogenes or Santa Claus. But as I seem to have been given his daughter's address should expect he is (or has been) in existence and not just a myth like one or more of previous parties named might be."* Though Perley never had any business dealings with Mr. MacBean, his humor achieved a better result. He and Miss MacBean continued corresponding for several years.

It was becoming common knowledge around town that despite his eccentricities, Perley was a shrewd businessman. Knowing there was talk circulating about him, Perley now considered this gossip something of a compliment. *"The story was around town that I lived on hedgehogs and blueberries and spent all my money in buying land."* Actually, this statement was not far from the truth. Though he often professed his dislike of killing,(*"Not much of a hunter, too tenderhearted. Perhaps on account of the name being so near feminine"*) it didn't seem to bother Perley to decapitate hedgehogs for the fifty cent bounty the town placed on their heads. Taught not to waste anything, Perley would first cut out the liver to fry up and eat; he would then feed the rest of the carcass to cats or foxes living nearby.

Living such a frugal life, Perley was able to accumulate money quickly. In one of his letters he shows how carefully he counted his pennies: *"For breakfast I had a can of fourteen cent chicken vegetable soup, with a couple of slices of nineteen cent raisin bread, and opened a ten cent can of spaghetti. But cookies, candy and coffee will perhaps make my day's board somewhere between thirty and forty cents."*

After Florence Brooks Aten was forced out of her home in 1929, Perley never held a regular job again. *"I was only a one horse farmer and day laborer, working hard for a living, till I turned 'hermit' and survived a little better without working."* But his foresight to buy land when it was being sold for post-depression prices of one to four dollars an acre ultimately enabled him to become the largest resident landowner and the fifth largest overall landowner in Stoddard with holdings totaling 1200 acres by 1953. Including acreage owned in surrounding towns, Perley had amassed an estate of over 2000 acres of land. *"It seems my income was likely to be over twice as much now [from sales of land] without working as it used to be when I were working about 60 hours a week."*

Perley felt vindicated by his success as a landowner. This had been his plan all along when his marriage and his family had still been together. He always believed he could make a better living investing in land than working for a paycheck.

He also was a firm advocate of fairness in his business dealings, and not merely fairness for himself. In one case, Perley had surmised that a parcel of land he was interested in buying was not worth the asking price and offered the seller, Mr. Burnham, fifty dollars less. Mr. Burnham reluctantly accepted the reduced deal. Perley eventually sold more pine off the property than he expected and his profit, when he resold the property, far exceeded his expectations. Perley promptly sent Mr. Burnham a check for fifty dollars with the message, *"Having sold the land I got of you at considerable profit, I feel it right and proper to give you the fifty dollars you took off from the price you were asking for it."* Not only did Perley send him the fifty dollars but he added another thirty for "interest." This same scenario happened at least two other times, always to the amazement and gratitude of the recipient.

The rest of Perley's income was earned in whatever way he could find to make a few dollars. Blueberries were still plentiful on his former farm, which he continued to rent out.

Perley set up a 'pick-your-own' business, relying on people's honesty (sometimes to his dismay) to drop their money in a jar.

After Elsie Jane died, Perley began selling off 'antiques' from the house for whatever dollars they would bring in. Anyone that happened by and showed an interest could make Perley an offer and walk away with a treasure. He had no qualms about selling family heirlooms. Though this annoyed Perley's siblings, who felt he had no right to sell off items which had belonged to their mother and, in turn, should be passed down to all her children; Perley did not feel he was under any such obligation.

One New York man bought *"well over one hundred dollars worth of antiques - bottles, iron kettles, sap buckets, baby carriage and crib."* Another person bought a parlor stove and spinning wheel and still another paid sixteen dollars for the old telephone (which had been replaced with a high-tech 'dial' phone) and a small chair.

One day a Boston banker happened by and offered Perley thirty dollars for an old Edison phonograph he had. Perley said he'd think about it. He then contacted his sister, Ella, who had "mostly" owned it years earlier, and asked if they should sell it, splitting the thirty dollars. Ella agreed and Perley sent her fifteen dollars. When the Boston banker returned several weeks later, Perley decided he might do better and raised the price to forty dollars which was accepted and paid.

Now Perley had a dilemma. Should he share the extra profit with Ella who had been only too happy with the original deal? Or should he keep the money himself as a just reward for smart negotiation? He settled the ethical quandary by giving the additional ten dollars away. *"Not being interested in churches, hospitals or other charities"* he chose to send it to a "girlfriend" he was writing to named Gladys. Her father was out of work and the family was having a difficult time making ends meet. Gladys and her family were so appreciative and wrote back with such praise for his generosity that Perley was stunned. This act of charity and the appreciation it earned him affected many of his financial decisions in the years to come.

Knowing it was inevitable that hunters would invade his property, Perley charged them a "tax" of twenty-five cents a day, or one dollar for the entire year (women were allowed to hunt for free). One year he made forty dollars from these fees. And these hunters provided most of the human contact he had during the lonely winter months when they would stop in to visit and warm up. One asked Perley if he ever saw a doctor. It only took him a second to reply, *"Yep, usually see a couple every hunting season."*

During hunting season Perley would try to keep his goats locked in the barn so as not to have them mistaken for deer by inexperienced hunters. Inevitably, some escaped confinement and put themselves at risk. One year, toward the end of the season, two Massachusetts hunters were traipsing around in the woods behind Perley's barn. They had been out all day with no luck and the temperature had been dipping in and out of the single digits. Ready to call it quits they started to head back to their truck when they caught a movement through the trees. Being "city slickers" who had probably never seen a deer in the wild, they raised their rifles and dropped their targets with one shot each. Quite proud of themselves, they walked over to retrieve their prizes.

It wasn't until they stepped into the clearing where the goats lay in a pool of blood, that they saw Perley calmly walking toward them, writing in a small notebook. Amazed that someone could have come upon them so quickly and quietly, the hunters just stood gaping. Without a word Perley handed each hunter a bill made out for 'damages', "One goat

- $20.00." The hunters pulled out their wallets and, without a fuss, paid Perley his forty dollars.

As they turned to leave, Perley called out, *"Don't you want to take them with you?"*

"Well, no," the hunters replied, feeling quite foolish over their error in judgment.

"I can bury them for you, I suppose, be another $5.00 a piece." Perley said as he kicked at the ground, *"Almost frozen now, won't be easy."* The hunters paid the extra ten dollars and hurried away.

What gave Perley the biggest chuckle when he would retell the story was that he had run out of meat and needed to kill one of his goats...but just didn't have the heart to do it. The hunters had done his work for him and also paid for the privilege of doing so.

Like most people, Perley had a distaste for filling out income tax returns and having to pay taxes on the little money he earned. Even with his land investments he seldom made enough income to file a tax return, usually keeping his annual income after deductions under the required $1,200.

When Perley reluctantly decided to sell his 220 acre home farm in Sullivan, where he had once lived with his wife and children, for just under six thousand dollars, he had to pay a tax of $176.33 on the profit over and above the $700 he had paid for it almost fifty years before. Though he wrote a poetic complaint to the Internal Revenue Service, Perley was still required to pay the tax. An I.R.S. agent showed up at Perley's door, *"with orders direct from Washington"* to take Perley to the city of Keene so he could withdraw the money from his bank to pay his taxes. Then the agent was to return Perley to his home.

After the transaction was over and the agent had Perley's taxes in hand, Perley asked if they might stop at a store while he picked up a few supplies. The agent quickly agreed, probably assuming Perley needed to pick up a few staples such as milk and eggs. The agent then watched as store personnel made several trips back and forth to load up his car with five cases of canned milk, three cases of Campbell's soup, several fifty pound bags of potatoes, and about a hundred pounds of other groceries. Perley's slight revenge was complete when he insisted a bad back would not allow him to carry all those groceries into his house (the agent had no choice) but he made sure he thanked the government agent profusely for his help.

Perley did receive a letter one day from "Uncle Sam" that actually made him quite happy. He explained in detail: *"It seems there were about three hundred people in N.H. entitled to monthly checks, under a new law, even if never worked under social security. I apparently qualified, as got no pension or welfare aid and income considered too small to live on. Our generous 'Uncle' wants everyone to have plenty of food, and being to blame for high prices, feels duty bound to aid the old people so to have no poverty in the USA."*

Perley was now eligible to receive thirty-five dollars a month in social security payments. Considering he could live on less than one dollar's worth of food a day, this would easily cover his monthly grocery bill. *"The government classed me as 'retired,"* Perley wrote, *"but I never had anything to retire from."* Offered the chance to receive extra insurance protection, over the included Medicare, for an additional three dollars a month, Perley declined. When he was finally issued his social security card, it was made out to "Taylor Pond Hermit."

Townspeople were beginning to take more notice of Perley for his unique and solitary lifestyle. Enough time had passed and people's memories were short. Neighbors who had made up their minds against him and blamed him for sins allegedly committed against his wife and family now attributed his eccentricities to his age rather than an odd nature. Rumors did persist about the 'old hermit' who lived alone in the woods with his goats, to be sure. But instead of ridicule, the tone of the gossip had turned toward acceptance of Perley as a local "character." The descriptor "hermit" was applied more and more frequently. In explaining his sometimes questionable behavior, Perley wrote that he was only *"living up to the reputation given me called "eccentric" by some and even more correctly by others, a "hermit." Am not offended if called nothing worse."*

Perley often said that the incident which sparked all the attention he would receive in the coming years was his refusal of a transistor radio his nephew, Russell Ball, had tried to give him. Russell had brought the radio to Perley as a Christmas present, a 'thank you' gift for letting him use a farm tractor which Perley owned but couldn't run. Russell had borrowed it to haul his winter's supply of firewood and wanted to show his appreciation. Because the radio was quite expensive for the time, Perley felt it was too extravagant a gift and would not accept it. The reason he gave, besides the expense, was that if he was tempted to listen to music or news, *"my poor goats might not be cared for properly."*

The local newspaper caught wind of this story and published a small article entitled, *"Hermit guards his 'standing."* The article went on to say that Perley refused the radio *"on the grounds that it would hurt his standing as a hermit"* and quoted him as saying *"I wouldn't be much of a hermit if I had a new-fangled gadget like that."*

Life didn't change much for Perley immediately after this first bit of publicity. Relatives teased him about his "hermit" status and he received a few pieces of mail from local strangers interested in his lifestyle. After a few weeks Perley thought his "fifteen minutes of fame" was over. Little did he know that within the next few years people as far away as California would be reading about him.

Perley's social security card
Made out to "Taylor Pond Hermit"

Perley Swett
Courtesy of Ernie Hebert

Chapter Sixteen
Perley's Poetry

In the lonely hours of his evenings, with only the glow of a kerosene lamp to pierce the darkness, Perley would take pencil and paper in hand, hunker down in his chair behind his table and write the poetry he hoped one day would be published. As he often said, *"Fame as a poet would carry greater honor than as a hermit. To be a famous hermit all you need to do is live alone and not die."*

Though he always strove to be known as a poet, perhaps it would be more accurate to describe Perley as a prolific writer. For writing in one form or another was therapy for Perley...a way to order the chaos of his rambling ideas into an acceptable rhythm of words. He seemed to think it added credence to his arguments to see them in print. Poetry was his way to be heard. And being heard was the way to be vindicated.

His accumulated diaries and journals filled over sixty booklets of varying sizes. These journals detailed his daily activities but were devoid of much emotion. They were simply an accounting of his day-to-day life. It was in his letters and poetry that he poured out his inner frustrations with a world that was too often cruel and unfair.

Despite his physical withdrawal from society after his release from the county farm, Perley maintained written contact with a number of relatives and acquaintances. Even strangers who caught Perley's attention received letters from him. One example was the Gillette family from Athens, Ohio, whose story appeared in an article in 1950 in *Grit*, a magazine devoted to rural life. Printed since 1882, *Grit* had a national circulation, offering lighthearted glimpses of rural life. (Within a few years Perley would be reading about himself in the same magazine.) What caught Perley's eye was the title: *"Ohio woman has 11th daughter one day before 35th birthday."* Mrs. Mary Gillette had just given birth to her eleventh consecutive girl, all born singly within a fifteen year span. Perley was so impressed with this accomplishment that he wrote to Mrs. Gillette requesting a picture of all the girls. His comment to her was, *"Believe you have the right idea in raising only girls and if all others followed your example it might be one solution to eliminate wars between nations."*

Perley and Mrs. Gillette continued to exchange letters for several years. Periodically, Perley sent a few dollars as gifts for her daughters. Perhaps Perley's friendship brought Mrs. Gillette good luck. Or perhaps not. The following year Mrs. Gillette broke her 'streak' when she gave birth to her twelfth and last child, a boy!

Perley composed his longwinded letters in pencil. Luckily he chose to preserve the hundreds of letters he wrote by making carbon copies. His own personal filing system, which consisted of placing these copies between pages of catalogues and magazines, helped protect them in the ensuing years. By also saving all the letters he received, Perley left behind a chronological accounting of a colorful life. This correspondence reveals not only his eccentricities but also his dry sense of humor.

But it was poetry that was Perley's favorite outlet for self expression. And it was poetry that allowed him to identify with his distant cousin, John Greenleaf Whittier.

But perhaps inherited the inclination verse to write,
As a cousinship to the "Quaker Poet" can be claimed;
Evening composing helps also to shorten a winter night,
Preferring to be as poet, more than hermit, famed.

Though Perley had fought against his sons continuing their education, he always regretted never having had the opportunity to further his own. Having quit school in the fifth grade, he often referred to himself as "just a poor, uneducated farmer." Yet he acted very much the opposite. Early in his life, Perley set himself apart from his equally uneducated siblings, friends and neighbors as a man to be respected...a man of letters. He always assumed poetry would be his path to recognition, the way to rise above his meager circumstances. Not wanting to appear "uneducated" he kept his dictionary handy to make sure he never made a mistake in his spelling. Ironically he seemed willing to sacrifice grammatical correctness - if he ever knew it - for poetic license. Perley always made his own rules.

Unfortunately for Perley, the more than three hundred (known) poems that he wrote in his lifetime would produce little literary recognition and no income. In yet another poem he lamented,

Poets and writers turn professional if at all,
By receiving payment for something wrote;
In the amateur class of unknown poets I fall,
And graduation prospects are yet remote.

My schooling were only that legally required,
I may as well to this error of judgment confess;
Very small income is now got from this land,
And for my poetry I have written, even less."

PERLEY'S POETRY

In a reply to a letter sent to him by an admirer of his poetry, Perley questioned the meaning behind her sentiments: *"Not sure of your meaning calling my writing ability 'priceless,"* he inquired, *"Fully realize my poetry is* [priceless], *as never were able to get any published, let alone to get any money for it."*

As is true of most poets, Perley wrote about what he experienced. But being self-centered and having very little exposure to the outside world, the topic that Perley knew best, and wrote about most, was himself. Writing about his problems may have been cathartic for Perley, but it prevented his poetry from appealing to a larger audience. Most of his compositions were long monologues of rhyming self-pity, many repeating the same despondent themes year in and year out. Of the many poems he wrote, only a few dealt with anything other than his view of himself as victim. One has to wonder what Perley could have accomplished with his gift for words had he been able to let go of his demons.

When asked by a young lady to write a poem about the "Beautiful Springtime," Perley was hard-pressed to come up with anything good to say. Perley's glass, metaphorically, was half empty at best:

"The snow is mostly gone, and brooks and rivers are now carrying the water away,
Springtime is here, but far less welcome than some city poets would seem to say.
Mud too deep for cars to get here, and swarms of flies, all seeking a chance to bite,
A "birthday poem about beautiful spring" it seems is what your suggestion was to have this poet write.

It cannot be done, it would be a lie, for spring is the very worst season of the year.

*Even though it displaced zero weather and deep snow, it
    brings no comfort here.
Perhaps in some sections of the country, spring may not be
    considered very bad;
But our poor ancestors, that settled New Hampshire, took the
    cheapest land that was then it seems to be had.*

*This old hermit's education is not good enough to tell of
    beauty that seems not to exist;
City poets might do much better, as perhaps all the discomforts of spring, they missed.
Seemingly a few weeks in the early fall, aids somewhat to
    make life worth living;
But the rest of the year can be given no praise unless other
    poets can do the giving.*

In time Perley's lonely lifestyle would lead him to ridicule - in verse - even the celebrated poetry of his idol and distant cousin, John Greenleaf Whittier. He compared Whittier's romantic tour de force, "Snowbound," to the life he was living at Taylor Pond as follows:

"Snow Bound or Stoddard History in Verse" [in part]

*The title of Whittier's poem I have here taken,
    But being related he doubtless would not care;
For a snow covered scene kindred hearts awaken,
    Even though a difference of opinion they share.*

*The fences like in John's story, are well covered,
    And the white drifts piled high all around;
Should death come how long before it were discovered,
    Deeply snowed in and completely "snowbound."*

Perley's Poetry

Were my cousin alone and blocked in so tightly,
  In that poem more of worry may have shown;
Though admitting the clean snow is very sightly,
  Often too much with a shovel must be thrown.

With a barn and house on speaking terms only,
  And up to four feet all the way snow between;
In that section of a township now wild and lonely,
  Two miles from a neighbor and no house to be seen.

Once by neighbors these old timers were surrounded,
  Within my memory the last half have slowly gone;
Sheep, cows and oxen in large number abounded,
  But the farms were deserted as the old folks passed on.

Perhaps no one about this desertion is complaining,
  If now other jobs and better locations are preferred;
Yet wild life with the woods and brush is gaining,
  With both bear and panther seen at times or heard.

The last resident in this district were my mother,
  My father was older and twenty years had been dead;
Now I try to farm this place rather than another,
  Where a spring breeze leveled my barn and shed.

A good path to travel is always badly needed,
  Between water at house and barn where it never flow;
Doubtless such matters were forgot or unheeded,
  In those verses telling of the drifted white snow.

But I heard that poem helped John G. get started,
  Less perhaps to wealth than the road to fame;
Maybe too much snow has made me downhearted,

Perley

And as I feel, must need write the same.

No claim do I make as a poet, or expect ever to see,
My name added to a list who are as poets classed;
So what I write may be forgot, as I expect to be,
Before all those now living from this life have passed."
[full version of poem in Perley's Poetry]

One hundred years earlier, in 1845, Henry David Thoreau decided to experience a solitary and simple existence by setting up a cabin in the woods by Walden Pond in Concord, Massachusetts. His experiment lasted two years, two months and two days. And though it helped him to produce some of his most famous literature, this "simple life" was never intended to be permanent. Although he said years later, *"Perhaps if I lived there much longer, I might live there forever,"* when he was ready to move on, Thoreau gave up his small cabin in the woods to move back into town with friends who, in fact, were never far away. Perley, however, never considered that was a viable option.

In the book, *Henry David Thoreau, Writer and Rebel*, by Philip Van Doren Stern, the author described Thoreau as a man who preferred the loneliness of the quiet countryside to the company of his fellow man. And though Thoreau could be critical of society, as was Perley, neither were the curmudgeons they appeared to be. *"Behind the mask was a highly sensitive person who wanted to avoid being hurt."* Like Perley, Henry David Thoreau's apparent indifference to others seemed linked to the fact that his own standards of a man's actions were so high that few of his contemporaries could meet those requirements. Perley and Henry David Thoreau also shared another similarity, a stubborn refusal to bow to authority when they felt their cause was just. Henry

David refused to pay his poll tax for several years in protest against a government that permitted slavery. In 1846 his actions finally caught up with him and he was arrested. The town constable even offered to pay what Thoreau owed but Henry insisted he be arrested, saying: *"It's the principle of the thing."*

But Thoreau only spent one night in jail. His tax was paid during the night by an unknown person. Thoreau, much like Perley, did not want to go free. He felt he was there on principle and intended to stay to prove his point. The jailer would not allow this, however, and forced Henry to leave. This one night in jail prompted Thoreau to write his widely read political essay "On the Duty of Civil Disobedience." To Perley's dismay, his writings during the more than three years he spent behind bars never achieved such broad social relevance or respect.

Another of America's great poets, Emily Dickinson, was also known for her life of self-imposed social seclusion. Because she chose to live a life of simplicity it created an aura of romanticized speculation around her. Though sharing this lifestyle with Perley, Emily had first attended college. She also continued to stay in contact with many influential and educated people she had met. Emily's decision to live life as a recluse did not close her mind to the wonders of life but in many ways her solitary existence allowed the flow of new thoughts and ideas which she ultimately recorded in her poetry.

It might seem presumptuous for this author to discuss her grandfather in the company of illustrious American writers such as Whittier, Thoreau and Dickinson. The point to be made, however, is not to compare the quality of their writing but about the circumstances that led up to it. Many authors choose seclusion for the quiet reflection that nurtures the writing process. Perley chose seclusion with a much different objective in mind, that of setting a barrier between himself and a society that he feared would not accept him. That seclusion also led to a flood of words. But his poetry was not a vehicle for entertainment or elucidation for others. Instead his poetry was the means by which his primal screams could be heard.

And Perley continually tried to find a wide audience for his laments. In 1949, he sent a long-winded tirade to the Reader's Digest on the evils of society and, in particular, what he viewed as a failed court system and its crooked lawyers. Surely the magazine would be happy to publish his weighty observations for the benefit of its readers. The editor kindly wrote back with the comment, *"The material you sent recently does not quite fit our needs."*

Still more poems using his fondness for legalese were devoted to the future disposition of his assets. In May of 1950, Perley composed a lengthy will, one that would be the first in a series of more than twenty he would write in his lifetime. Subsequent poetic revisions were deemed necessary not only to deal with the growth and complexity of his estate but also with his on again/off again relationships with his friends and family and, particularly, his children who might, or might not be designated as his heirs.

Finally, a discussion of Perley's poetry would not be complete without mentioning one group of poems that departed dramatically from his central theme of social injustice. These were the many love poems he composed to women who caught his eye. Though it was questionable that he ever seriously considered a second marriage, he enjoyed dreaming about the possibility. And if his flowery poetry were to be taken literally, one could assume he was not averse to the possibility of a little hanky panky!

PERLEY'S POETRY

*I am now old, and fast growing older, and must perhaps still
  live a hermit's life,*
*And long ago had given up expectation, and all hope, of ever
  getting another wife;*
*But I would surely appreciate a little love, and often wish I
  could at least feel,*
*How it would seem to now have an angel sleeping beside me,
  one that is near to my ideal.*

For many years, Perley signed not only his poetry but also his personal letters as Pearl Whittier. One has to wonder if he was hoping to cash in on his cousin's fame, did not feel that the name Perley Swett was "literary" enough or simply liked the cachet of having a pen name. Possibly, fearing that his writings might bring further rejection, Perley felt safer operating behind a façade. But why choose one of a feminine nature?

It appeared more and more likely that Perley's one claim to fame was not going to result from being known as an acclaimed poet, a shrewd land dealer or as an honest businessman. He was discovering that his fame was growing not from his contributions *to* society but from his withdrawal *from* society. Rather than fight this fact, Perley chose to encourage this persona and polish it for the world to see. Perhaps fame as a hermit was better than no fame at all. Perley finally wholeheartedly embraced the title, no longer signing his letters or poetry as Pearl Whittier, the poet, but as "The Hermit of Taylor Pond."

Perley in his doorway with hand made sign
Courtesy of Elva Swett Frazier

Chapter Seventeen
Paradise Found and Paradise Lost

In 1953, Yankee Magazine of Dublin, New Hampshire, decided to do an article about the hermit that lived in the back woods of the town of Stoddard. The editor of the magazine had heard about Perley and decided to see what potential there was for a story. He sent two reporters to find and interview the hermit.

As the men made their slow progression over several miles of rutted wagon path through the woods, the trees suddenly gave way to an open meadow splashed with golden sunshine. *"Is this the end of the road?"* one of the reporters asked as Perley stepped out of his house. *"Has been for many years for me, lad,"* was Perley's profound reply.

Perley agreed to be interviewed for the article. Entitled "The Hermit of Devil's Paradise," it related the reporters' impressions of the hermit and his homestead: *"It was a lonely place. In the silence of it all only the call of a goat to its young was apparent. But there was time - and peace - in which to realize this had not always been so. Stage coaches, a hundred years ago, had used the old county highway as a main route. The farms were prosperous then. Wonderful people had grown up on them - had gone out into the world to make it a much better place for all.*

"The Hermit had some solace in the realization of how he alone was now the only defender man had against Nature in

this struggle to maintain the highway and home of his forefathers. He told us he hoped it would be opened clear through to Stoddard again some day - for the sportsman, the summer resident, the wild life lover, as an unspoiled New Hampshire countryside."

After the interview, as the Yankee reporters were reluctantly preparing to leave, one of them asked Perley, *"So...you find happiness here and in this fashion?"* This direct question met with an equally direct answer as Perley summed up his life in a negative nutshell. *"Son, I will never be happy anywhere. I have seen too many of the world's troubles. People are rotten. Out here, the thing is, at least they leave me alone. That's all I ask."*

The Yankee reporter ended his article with his own summation of Perley's life: *"In common with some people everywhere he had more than once been cheated, imposed upon, hurt and disillusioned. In this he was reacting no differently perhaps than many another sensitive soul whose end of the road has held less, rather than more, intimacy with people. Some have retired behind cocktails, bridge, golf, hobbies, careers, even public life. The Hermit's choice is his family's lonely hilltop farm. The philosophical conclusion is the same - only the address is different."* (Reprinted with permission from Yankee Publishing Inc.)

Though he was not identified by name in the article, it was not difficult for local townspeople to discern who the piece was about. Word traveled quickly and Perley became an instant celebrity. New residents in the town had not even been aware that Perley lived deep in their woods. Only the old timers were aware of Perley's past. Others may have recalled that there had been some dark tales whispered about him but the details were fuzzy. This only added to his mystique.

As 'the Hermit of Devil's Paradise' Perley was beginning to feel much more appreciated by society. He still had his privacy, especially in the winter months, but he did not feel quite as secluded. More and more often people braved his dirt road to visit the hermit and his goats.

However, the attention waxed and waned and it wasn't until another round of publicity came several years later that 'the Hermit of Taylor Pond' would be transformed from local curiosity to well-known personage, not just locally but nationally. As Perley later said, *"Can't believe I made the news all the way to the Pacific Coast."*

In the meantime, the 1960s were just around the corner. Perley now had twenty-two grandchildren and four great-grandchildren. Though he seldom saw them it was due more to the difficulty of traveling an all but impassable road rather than lack of interest. The passage of time had healed some family wounds and Perley enjoyed his grandchildren, holding no grudge against them.

Though he was in excellent health given his age, Perley could feel his mortality creeping up on him. At age seventy-two, he wrote that having *"Four great grandchildren have made me feel so old I do not try to walk to Munsonville anymore, as my legs get enough exercise just going to the barn, and don't like to trust them for a six mile walk."*

Perhaps one event, more than any other, made Perley realize that time was marching on...and that its direction was not reversible. Perley heard through the grapevine that his former employer, neighbor and friend, Florence Brooks-Aten, had passed away.

Perley had kept up an infrequent correspondence with Florence during their later years even though they never did visit in person again. The theme of their letters was always the same: bemoaning the loss of happier times.

"I often look back to those years," Florence wrote, *"so long ago when I was able to help many and was happy there where I could share with friends and neighbors. Now all is*

changed and I can only make a cake or do the simple things for neighbors and friends and then not often. I do get very depressed as I am so alone now. Money never meant much to me, it never gave me real happiness. It did make me happy to share it and do with it the things that brought relief and happiness to those I loved. I am very changed because I have no great ambitions and am satisfied with a clean room and home comforts."

Florence Aten was one of the last connections Perley had with his previous life. It had been over forty years since she first fell in love with a two acre lot at Wood's Mill. Perley had seen her through the building of her approximately twelve hundred acre estate. And after the 1929 Crash, Perley had watched as ownership of her land changed hands many times in the ensuing years.

Initially, after Florence lost the property, it was sold in auction to T.L.MacBean of New York City. After MacBean finished logging the property for the timber value, he sold it to partners Kasper Klatsky and Edward Murphy. In 1957 Edward L. Parker, a Miami real estate developer acquired the land and buildings in the name of "New Hampshire Lakeshores, Inc." He broke down Florence's property into 435 lots of approximately one-eighth of an acre each. Only sixty-nine lots were ever sold. The developer fled when the illegal dam he had constructed on Chandler Meadow was bulldozed by the state. In 1962 the unsold property went to tax auction once again. Earl Batchelder was the only bidder and bought the property for a whopping $362. [It wasn't until the turn of the century, in 2001, almost eighty years after it was begun, that Florence's home was finally bought by someone who lovingly restored it to its original intent - See "A Final Visit"].

Perley and Florence were a study in contrasts. Perley was born into poverty and, from childhood on, labored long hours to escape from it. Florence, accustomed to privilege from birth, grew into adulthood with no compulsion to save for her future. To achieve his ends, Perley hoarded every penny he could earn. Florence spent her inheritance freely, confident that she would always have ample means to make her personal world, and the world at large through her philanthropy, a better place. Life's encounters led Perley, ultimately, to trust no one. Florence's life of comfort led her to trust others far too much. And while Perley was becoming more and more obsessed with achieving financial security, Florence gave no thought to her own fortune...until it was too late.

That these two polar opposites would chance to meet, or indeed develop a close bond, is truly remarkable...until one considers the land, the *place* where they hoped to realize their dreams. The Whittier homestead on Taylor Pond was hardly the best farm land to be found in southwestern New Hampshire. And an abandoned saw mill site at Wood's Mill was an unlikely location for an elegant Adirondack lodge and estate. Yet these largely uninhabited and wild expanses of land abutting each other in the hills of Stoddard were the canvasses each chose to paint their life portraits. Their reasons for choosing this area were certainly quite different but both were equally committed to this *place* they called home.

One can ponder the different courses both Perley and Florence took that led to their lonely lifestyles, but one has to be struck by the realization that this unlikely but compelling place played such a role. This humble ground would leave a rich woman impoverished and enable a poor man to achieve wealth above his station. And while Perley would never leave his land because of the comfort and protection it afforded him, Florence would never return to her's despite living the last twenty years of her life within fifteen miles of Wood's

Mill. They would each end their lives as isolated from society as the land that had shaped their destiny.

Before she died and in a moment of cold reflection, Florence wrote to Perley, *"we make such a fuss over our short and puny lives and when we leave we are soon forgotten."* Sadly, Florence had already been forgotten. When she passed away on July 20, 1960 from a heart attack at age eighty-five, she had no people around her. Her body lay undiscovered for days in her small cottage on Wilson Pond at the edge of Keene.

Perley remembered Florence in the only way he could express his grief, in his poetry. But his sorrow was not about the loss of a close friend and neighbor. Instead it was about something that meant much more to him, land and the loss of a dream.

"Wood's Mill of the future, for you what has God in store?
 And Wood's Mill Manor you are called, t'was Shinbone Shack before,
A mansion large and stately, a garden with stonewalls in the sun,
 Was built beside your waters, but never quite got done."
  The Unfinished Dream
   (full poem in Perley's Poetry)

1953 Article from Yankee Magazine about Perley
Reprinted with permission from Yankee Publishing Co.

Florence Brooks Aten sitting on her porch at
Shinbone Shack - Taken around 1925
Courtesy of Charlie Wilder

Chapter Eighteen
A Final Resting Place

When Florence Brooks Aten died, the authorities did not know what should be done with her body. She had left no instructions about where or even if she wanted to be buried. None of her neighbors knew of any living relatives. Finally, after some searching, it was discovered that a son, Albert, was living in Reading, Vermont. When contacted he directed that his mother's body be sent to a crematorium in Springfield, Massachusetts. Whether he ever collected his mother's ashes is unknown. It was years later that a headstone was finally erected in the Ellwanger family plot in Rochester, New York as a final remembrance of Florence.

Realizing that he could find himself in the same precarious predicament, Perley knew he needed to make some definite plans.

One of Perley's earliest memories was of standing by the edge of a small hand-dug grave as his father carefully placed the pine box holding the body of his beloved baby brother, Luman Frederick, into the ground. The mound of dirt soon grassed over but was not forgotten. From time to time Perley would stand over the site and talk to his brother. And he knew that when his own time came, he wanted to keep his little brother company on the family farm.

Perley was worried, and rightfully so, that if he did not leave specific instructions for what he wanted done when he died, he would spend eternity not on his land but in a distant cemetery. He turned again to poetry to express his feelings on the matter:

"Both parents died in this old house, one grandfather too, as well as a small younger brother,
Graves aplenty on this old farm, though in cemeteries, among other dead, some preferred to lie;
This hermit has long lived here alone, and wants his last resting place near no other,
Marked only by a natural stone, roughly inscribed, to tell passing strangers the date he die."

But merely stating his wishes poetically might not carry enough weight. He needed to take action.

Perley walked his land for days looking for the perfect spot. He finally settled on a shaded area at the north edge of the woods overlooking his home. It was, indeed, marked by a huge granite boulder as well as a grove of birch trees. He began to dig his own grave.

This was an arduous task for a seventy-four year old man of slight stature. Undisturbed for decades, the ground was unyielding. Almost a month was spent removing small shovelfuls of dirt, cutting and pulling roots and removing rocks of all sizes from the ground until Perley felt the hole was of sufficient size. Then he smoothed the sides of the excavation and supported them so they wouldn't collapse. Because he *"never did learn to swim,"* Perley rigged a drainage system to allow the ground water to run off, keeping the hole dry. It took most of that summer but finally his grave was ready for occupancy. Now no one could question his wishes for a final resting place. His bond with his land was sealed for eternity.

He then turned his attention to selecting an appropriate epitaph, finding *"I still haven't decided what I want to say about myself."* Choosing a date of death was also problematic, Perley conceded, *"The Good Lord hasn't mentioned it yet."* Though there had been times when he felt his life was not worth living, Perley was not willing to give it up just yet. Not by a long shot. The date he settled on was November 26, 2013, which would have made him 125 years old when he died! *"I figure I'm going to live just as long in the next century as I did in the last,"* Perley explained.

For a grave marker Perley used a fourteen foot barn board on which he wrote with a can of roofing tar, "2-6-1888 Taylor Pond Hermit 11-26-2013." Local author Ernest Hebert recalls visiting Perley that summer with a college friend. *"As Perley showed us his intended gravesite, I asked him if he really expected to die on that date."* Mr. Hebert remembered Perley's reply with amusement, *"He said, 'Either then or before.'"*

It seems quite poignant that Perley chose to identify his final resting place not with his name, but with a label, "Taylor Pond Hermit." Perhaps he believed that <u>what</u> he was carried more importance than <u>who</u> he was. It was by this persona that he wished to be remembered.

> *"His grave is ready dug, by a large marked stone,*
>   *Where he wishes to rest while his bones rot away;*
> *Many years he has lived on this farm all alone,*
>   *And on this place of his birth, he desires forever*
>   *to stay"*

It didn't take long before Perley's grave-digging exploit became gossip for the townspeople. Soon another round of newspaper articles appeared, several were headlined: "The Hermit who dug his own grave." This time Perley had no qualms about letting his name be used. Several newspaper reporters interviewed him and wrote about his life. As he later told his youngest daughter, Bernice, by then married with ten children of her own, *"If I realized how much company I would get just by my digging a hole, I could have dug lots of holes before now."*

This new flood of publicity secured Perley's reputation as a bona fide media-friendly hermit. People were fascinated with this quirky recluse who lived alone in the woods and, in the mood of the 1960s, they envied Perley's freedom to live exactly as he desired. Perley began playing the role to perfection. Not only did he look every inch the hermit, with his ragged clothes and dilapidated house, he had the wit, the cynicism and the sense of humor to make it work. And what better way to cement one's image as a fascinating eccentric than to dig one's own grave!

The mail was coming in faster than he could answer it. *"My 'desk' is even more cluttered than usual,"* he pretended to complain. Asked to write a poem about dying, Perley demurred. *"Digging a grave did not mean I intended to use it right away. Among these Stoddard hills the air is not polluted by gas, smoke and disease germs, so may be here for the next fifty years (above the ground) before using the grave I dug. Sorry, but someone else may have the chance to compose a poem about 'dying alone in the Stoddard backwoods.' I can only write about things that have come to pass already."*

To another admirer he replied, *"Hope the 'excavation' remains 'untenanted' quite a few years yet. As I have told some people that even though Stoddard winters are cold, were in no hurry to pass on to a climate that might be less cold."*

During this episode in Perley's life, the more his reputation grew as a hermit, the less he actually lived like one. *"Not sure if I am a hermit except in winter time only. Since I got so "famous" have enough visitors in summer months so hardly believe can claim to be a year round hermit."* As his notoriety grew, still more newspaper articles were written about Perley further increasing visitations deep in the Stoddard woods. Hoping to meet him and capture a little reminder of what life was like a century before, people came with their cameras and their curiosity.

On these occasions Perley would call out to his goats to join him for a suitable "photo op" as soon as any vehicle pulled into his yard. Children and adults were surprised and charmed by Perley's approachability. Eager to be a good host, he kept cases of Saltines on hand for visitors to pass out to the goats. Children ran and played in the fields with the baby goats, climbed on the old treadmill or had their picture taken with the hermit. And Perley was only too happy to oblige.

At the end of each day, after company had left, Perley wrote in his journal about who came to see the "Famous Hermit" always putting this title in quotation marks as if he were talking about someone other than himself. Perhaps he imagined he was, for his life had turned into a performance and he had immersed himself in the part he was playing.

Perley found himself entering an era that actually applauded his "back to basics" lifestyle. The '60s decade brought with it its 'flower children' dressed in ragged clothing, long hair and beards, expressing a desire to live off the land. Perley was suddenly a symbol for societal dropouts. As a solitary figure given to spouting New England witticisms and poetry, Perley was what every Haight-Ashbury hippie aspired to be. Though he was still thought of as odd and eccentric, such qualities to many were now accepted and admired rather than ridiculed. Those that didn't know his sad story envied his lifestyle of simplicity and projected themselves into it. And though he often tried to explain his particular circumstances, people were content to believe that he was thumbing his nose at the "establishment," something that was very much in vogue at the time. The truth, however, as Perley clarified it, was: *"What made me a "famous hermit" was because I were too obstinate to leave the old rock farm when all my neighbors moved away and left me the only resident in a whole former school district."*

Townspeople were also jumping on the bandwagon. Suddenly residents of both Sullivan and Stoddard, who in the past took little notice of Perley, were now laying claim to him. Older residents who did not approve of Perley previously, now boasted that they knew him 'when' and simply winked at his past. Newcomers to the area were interested only in what Perley had become, not in where he had been.

Local publicity was picked up by newspapers and magazines across the country, spreading the notoriety of the Hermit of Taylor Pond. Even the New Hampshire Public Television channel did a short segment devoted to showing Perley and his lifestyle. He began getting fan mail from as far away as California: *"sent <u>airmail</u> but took four weeks to reach me as had to wait for someone to bring it up."* Perley was surprised by his new found stardom. *"Never expected I would be famous enough to have my picture in California papers."* Perley always sent a reply to any mail received, especially when it was from a woman. Upon receiving a perfumed piece of stationery, he wrote the young lady: *"I didn't identify the brand but it is different than the three kinds I am acquainted with - skunk, fox and billy goat."*

Perley had never found his "perfect mate," but he was suddenly attracting the interest of a great number of women for the first time in his life...and he was reveling in it! *"When one lady said my picture 'was not good' and wanted a better one sent,"* he told a visitor, *"I advised her I might try and look like a banker or insurance agent next summer but were not aware a hermit were supposed to 'furnish' pictures that would impress the ladies."*

Thinking him a romantic figure to flirt with, women of all ages would write and visit, hoping for a piece of poetry from the hermit to show to their friends. On such occasions Perley never failed to hand out copies of his earlier poem, "Housekeeper Wanted." Although he enjoyed the teasing and, in fact, gave as much as he received, he was puzzled by what he judged to be a genuine surge of interest in himself from the opposite sex. Retreating to his poetry to muse over his deepest feelings, he wrote:

It seems hard for this old hermit to understand,
 When young, and able to work, he searched the land,
Far and near, and no interested girl could he find,
 But now there are plenty when he is old and feeble
  and nearly blind.

He gets so many letters, he can hardly reply to all,
 Mostly girls between ten and twenty, both short
  and tall,
Just why did they wait till he were crippled and lame,
 But when he needed a 'housekeeper' most, none
  applied and none came.

1962 newspaper article reprinted
with permission from the Boston Herald

Perley's gravesite
"2-6-1888 Taylor Pond Hermit 11-26-2013"

Chapter Nineteen
Visitors - Wanted and Unwanted

To Perley's delight, not a week would go by during the summer without visitors stopping in to check on him. But that changed dramatically with the New Hampshire seasons. Until snowmobiles became popular in the late sixties, people had no way to travel miles of unplowed roads to Taylor Pond unless they chose to hike in on snowshoes. This meant reverting back to 'hermit status' for the long winter months. Not until June, when mud season was over, would Perley start receiving company again.

In 1965 a young lady by the name of Ellen Howard stumbled upon Perley's house one summer day as she was driving the back roads searching for abandoned cellar holes. Fascinated by local history and curious about old homes and the secrets they held, when Ellen came upon Perley's seemingly abandoned homestead she couldn't wait to investigate. She could only imagine who might have lived there at one time. As Ellen opened the door of her truck, she was startled by the sudden appearance of a strange old man holding a long stick in his hands. Perley raised his walking stick in greeting but took Ellen by such surprise that she quickly shut her door and drove back home for reinforcements. Several days later, with her mother and brother along for support, Ellen returned to Perley's. He cordially invited them in and they all had a good laugh about her previous swift departure. What followed was an enjoyable afternoon conversing with each other.

Ellen subsequently became a regular visitor of Perley's, taking him on errands into town or bringing him some of her mother's home-made beans and applesauce. At first, Perley was a bit suspicious of the friendly interest of this attractive young lady, finding it hard to believe that she could simply enjoy his company with no ulterior motives. But flattered by her attention, Perley soon became enthralled by his new "girlfriend." Normally preferring brunettes, he was willing to make a concession about her "lovely long blond hair" but when he confessed to Ellen his usual preference she had a confession of her own. She admitted that she colored her hair and was, in fact, a brunette. Though Perley was willing to overlook this small deception on Ellen's part, he considered it to be a slightly misleading practice.

In exchange for her kindnesses, Perley tried to return her favors whenever he could with small gifts. That Christmas season he allowed Ellen to cut several spruce trees off his property, Christmas trees for family and friends. With the trees loaded on her truck, she offered Perley a ride to Keene where he wanted to do some banking. As Ellen was helping Perley out of her truck, a man walked by and commented on the trees she had stacked in the back. *"I see you are getting all ready for Christmas,"* he said, and when he glimpsed Perley in his long winter beard and white hair, he continued, *"And you even have your very own Santa Claus too."*

Ellen had been attending college at Keene State after completing two years at the New England Conservatory in Boston. One day while telling him about life in the city, she realized that Perley had never been to Boston. She invited him to go with her to see the sights. Nervous about the prospect of experiencing something so completely out of his comfort zone, he nonetheless was excited to see the city where he knew his father, Daniel, had lived and worked in a machine shop as a mechanic when he was young. Dressed in his best clothes, Perley climbed into Ellen's red Volkswagon bug and headed for Boston.

Perley had many new experiences that day and seemed to enjoy them all. A wide eyed tourist, he and Ellen rode the elevator to the observation tower of the John Hancock building, *"my first ride in an elevator that went over two stories high."* They visited Jordan Hall at the Conservatory, a museum, "shopped" in a few stores and sat on a bench in Boston Common. They ate lunch at Ken's Delicatessen in Copley Square. Perley was energized by his day in the city but the hermit was tired and relieved when he returned that evening to the peace and quiet of his farm. Welcomed home by the goats, he wearily did his chores and retired early. Unfortunately, shortly after their Boston adventure, Ellen moved away to Florida but always made it a point to visit Perley whenever she was home for a visit.

Though contact with human beings was sporadic, his goats were his constant companions. It was the goats that broke his loneliness, giving each day a purpose. As he wrote to a friend, *"No one to feed and water the goats but me so it seems necessary to keep alive."*

Perley's only source of water was the well in the entryway to his house, which was two hundred feet from the barn. Perley made as many as ten or more trips to the barn daily, each time carrying two full buckets of water. This gave him an hour or more of exercise every day. *"If it were not for the necessity of caring for goats,"* he wrote, *"not sure as would get any exercise."* Perley described in a letter to a friend, *"Usually have to change twenty water dishes for them twice daily in order to live up to my "reputation"* [as described in a newspaper article] *of "tending my herd of goats with the care of a brood hen."*

Though he no longer bothered to make maple syrup, Perley still put out a few buckets in the spring to collect sap because the goats enjoyed drinking it.

Even with such meticulous care, Perley's goat herd was dwindling. From an all time high of 119, now he had less than half of that. Over the years, Perley had sold some goats, used some for meat and lost the rest to sickness, hunters or dogs. Once he suspected that a neighbor he was having trouble with over land purchases was killing some of his goats though he could never prove it.

In October of 1966, during one of his early morning treks to the barn, Perley encountered a scene that made his blood run cold. There were deep claw marks on the barn where a bear had tried to break in to get to the goats. The bear was unsuccessful that time. A large timber was blocking the window so it was unable to climb through. Realizing that a couple of young goats had not returned home in the last few days, Perley wondered if this bear already had had a chance to sample young goat meat and now wanted more.

Perley contacted his family and before long there were hunters swarming all over the area. *"Must have been perhaps more than 75 folks here one Sunday. Maybe 1/2 hunting for the bear, some just to see tracks in barn yard."*

Whether the commotion of the hunters scared off the bear or it went into hibernation, it was not seen again until the next spring. This time, hungry after a long winter's nap and remembering the availability of young goat meat, the bear was more aggressive and broke into Perley's barn and killed three of his goats who were trapped in their pens. It was heart-wrenching when Perley entered his barn and saw the bloody and chewed remains of his pets. He dragged the carcasses outside and away from the barn in the hope that if the bear did return it would be content with the remains.

Unfortunately, the bear had gotten a taste for fresh kill and ignored the leftovers. A few nights later another young goat went missing. Bloody tracks on the ground indicated where it had been dragged away. Realizing this bear would never leave as long as food was so readily available, Perley knew it would have to be killed.

He immediately called his son, Maurice who, in turn, contacted some professional hunters from Vermont. Four men came down with ten dogs to search for the bear. They wanted to use one of Perley's remaining goats as bait to attract the bear but Perley would have none of that as he knew how frightened the poor goat would be. *"I buried the remains of those three goats yesterday. I don't want to have to bury any more."*

Luckily the fresh tracks gave the dogs their scent, and they were able to locate the bear within an hour. Finding it up a tree, the hunters shot the bear which half climbed and half fell to the ground. Wounded, the bear was still able to give chase. Shots had to be fired carefully to avoid hitting the dogs which ran in a frenzy around the charging bear. It was only after pumping ten shots into the bear that it was finally stopped, just thirty feet from the hunters.

Perley's bear was killed on May 9, 1967, and was assumed to weigh between 225 and 275 pounds since it had just come out of a long winter hibernation. It was estimated it would have weighed between four to five hundred pounds at the end of the summer. The bear was cut in half for easier transport and Herbert Nims, a professional taxidermist in the area, mounted the bear's head and feet. For many years they hung in Maurice's living room.

It was with a good deal of trepidation that Perley looked back on his one and only encounter with a bear. *"The killer bear is dead, those three goats buried and I can only regret I did not realize how easily the bear could get in the barn. Perhaps lucky for me the barn is so far away from house that my first knowledge of what happened was going outdoors after daylight. If had heard it during the night and gone out to investigate, might not be here now to tell about it. It did look pretty, as it had a lovely black coat and seemed as large around as a barrel. First wild one I ever see."*

Ellen Howard and Perley
Taken February 1973

Perley doing chores
Courtesy of John Bridges

Perley pointing out bear tracks for Keene Sentinel reporter
Originally published in the Keene Sentinel October 5, 1966

Chapter Twenty
To Give is to Receive

The 19th Century philosopher, Soren Kierkegaard, observed that life, to be fully understood, must be viewed looking back on it. But unfortunately, we must live it going forward. It is doubtful that Perley ever read Kierkegaard but as he grew older Perley was indeed looking back on the road he had taken. *"Perhaps to ideas long outmoded I may too firmly have clung, but instilled so deep they could not seem to be outgrown."* And advancing age which idled daily chores gave him even more time to reflect on the meaning of his long journey. Land and more land had been the prize he had been chasing, and he had captured the prize. But what had it gained him? Perley's land had brought him moderate wealth - on paper - but few, if any, creature comforts. As he said with rancor, it *"might have been appreciated more if the 'taste of affluence' had come earlier instead of seeming so close to life's end."* More importantly, it had not brought him the love and companionship he had sought.

On February 6, 1968, Perley reached his eightieth birthday. It had become glaringly obvious that without assistance he would not be able to remain on the land where he was born...and hoped to die. His legs were no longer steady enough to carry him on long treks through the woods. His eyesight and hearing were failing and a touch of rheumatism in his shoulder often left him uncomfortable and sore.

He could no longer get to town for groceries or to handle financial matters, chores he had always attended to himself. He needed to ask for and accept help. And he was astonished to find that by doing this, others were more than willing to give it.

One such person was Quentin White, who along with his family, had just moved to New Hampshire where he had joined the faculty at Keene State College as a professor of geography. After weeks of searching, Quentin and his family rented a house on Granite Lake in Munsonville, three miles south of Taylor Pond. Quentin's family enjoyed exploring the woods around their new home and one of their expeditions resulted in their first encounter with Perley.

Quentin gave the following account of that day: *"It was a sunny day in the spring of 1969 and the kids wanted to go for a ride. We had a Volkswagon bus and decided to explore a little. We took Aten road on the northwest side of the lake. It was a beautiful ride and full of surprises. The first big one was the water wheel, bridge and dam at what I came later to know as "Shinbone Shack." We explored a little and walked around the old lodge wondering, with imagination, how and when it had all been constructed. It had kind of a fairy tale atmosphere and it drew us onward anxiously on unexplored roads to see what else there might be. It was exciting, especially to the children.*

We picked our way along wondering all the time if the trail would finally lead us to a dead end. There was no place to turn around so the anxiety built when suddenly the swamp ended. We turned right because the forest opened up that way. The road was immediately full of basketball size boulders as it went up hill. It was obviously a very old and deeply eroded road. As we got to the top of the short hill the landscape opened up into fields on both sides of the road and ahead on the left stood a terribly old vacant looking house with an equally old looking barn on the other side of the little road.

Within seconds Perley appeared at the front door and walked with his stick toward the road. The kids were ecstatic and I was flabbergasted! Perley was dressed in dirty tan pants and button-in-the-front underwear for a shirt, a costume that we learned was standard. His hair and beard were long and white. He waved his stick in greeting at us as we approached. I couldn't have been more amazed. We stopped and chatted with him. He was especially glad to see the children."

Perley invited Quentin and his children in and they all had a wonderful visit that afternoon. As they were leaving, Quentin asked Perley if there was anything he could do for him. Normally refusing such offers of help, Perley was down to a single can of Campbell's soup and a partial box of "soda" crackers and needed supplies badly. He asked if Quentin would mind going to town to shop for some needed items which Perley would, of course, pay for along with his gas. Glad to be of help, the White family purchased the items Perley had on his list and thus began a special friendship.

Touched by Quentin's kindness, wisdom and generosity, Perley grew to rely on him in the coming years. Perley couldn't have asked for a better or more loyal friend and even came to trust Quentin with financial matters, a huge leap of faith for Perley. Though Perley was more friendly and caring toward his own family now, and relied on many of them for their assistance around the farm, he seemed to be most comfortable turning to Quentin for help with business matters.

Quentin also helped Perley with less sophisticated chores. Perley liked to tell the story of how his barn was in dire need of having the manure shoveled out and clean straw brought in for the goats, chores Perley no longer could do himself.

Quentin offered his services and enlisted the aid of fellow professor, Klaus Bayr, to help with the unappealing job. Perley marveled at how he came to deserve the attention of two highly educated college professors who were willing to clean goat manure out of his barn. *"The only case, known to me, where an old one-horse farmer, without the horse, had such 'classy' help."*

Throughout his life Perley lived by his own code of conduct: he fully expected to work for his own keep and he fully expected that he should keep all that he had earned. He never asked for or expected charity and felt others should follow his example. Whenever favors were received from others they were repaid in kind. His relationships, both business and social, were always weighed on that balance until age began catching up with him. And while his body had become weak, his pride was as strong as ever. Instead of bartering favors and friendship with his own labor, he would now pay for them with hard cash.

However, looking at Perley in his ragged and dirty apparel and listening to the stories told about him, many people thought he was just a poor old farmer, down on his luck, living in a shack of a house with not a nickel to his name. It came as quite a surprise then when Perley would give money to those who helped or befriended him. Perley especially liked to give a few dollars to young children who visited with their families. Their parents, thinking Perley desperately needed every dollar he had, would try to refuse these gifts but Perley insisted.

As his generosity intensified, so did the rewards it produced. Not because of the amount he gave, but because he gave it freely. He was finally earning the admiration and affection that had eluded him for so long. And Perley was astounded to find that those who wished to help him were insistent that they wanted nothing in return except his friendship.

Perley never reached a point in his life where he could be considered rich. Though there was gossip to the contrary, he did not have mattresses stuffed with money. He had little use for cash because he lived so cheaply and *"never did learn how to spend money."* In earlier years he'd been intent on proving himself financially. Now he had no such need or desire. Any windfall profits he received for selling land, he immediately gave away. As he said, *"After I got to be 80 I hardly felt it necessary to continue saving for old age. My ordinary expenses being quite low and not being able to take it with me, anything above a safe reserve I always felt might as well be given to relatives or others that were both needing aid and worthy of receiving help."*

Perley remembered how good he felt when, after giving the money to his pen-pal Gladys and her family, he was then doubly rewarded by their gratitude. This was a new feeling, one that changed his life. He decided to look for more "needy and worthy" recipients. And his favorite beneficiaries were young ladies because he felt (call him chauvinistic, but his heart was in the right place)that they were less able to support themselves in a world where young men were more physically capable.

Perley had mentioned to Quentin that he wanted to donate some money to a person truly in need and wondered if Quentin's church could suggest someone. Not yet totally aware of Perley's financial status and assuming that one who lived so frugally must need the money himself, Quentin hesitated to assist Perley in his plans. But when Perley insisted he could afford it, Quentin suggested a young girl from Finland that he knew who was living with her mother in Utah and attending Brigham Young University.

Seija was crippled with arthritis and forced to spend most of her time in a wheelchair. Perley was sympathetic to her plight and began a correspondence with her. Admiring her determination, Perley told Quentin he wanted to help ease her burden by paying her rent for the next six months while she went to school, at the rate of ninety-dollars a month. Following Perley's instructions, Quentin arranged for payment to go directly to Seija's and her mother's landlord. Not being religious himself, Perley felt that arrangement was best because he did not want the women to feel obligated to pay a 'tithe' to the Mormon church out of his money. If the landlord chose to make such a donation, that was up to him. In addition to the rent money, Perley also sent another check for one hundred dollars to aid in the purchase of a car for young Seija. She and her mother wrote to Perley and gushed their gratitude once again, increasing his joy for having helped others in need.

Soon it became common practice for Perley to choose someone in need of aid that he either met or read about in the paper. *"They all had some sort of difficulty, accident or sickness, that touched his heart."* Quentin said. He would then ask Quentin, whom he considered "a completely honest man" to take him to the bank where Perley would secure a bank check (Perley never had a checking account himself). Then, much like the old television show, "The Millionaire," Perley would have Quentin deliver the check to the needy recipient.

Quentin recalled the usual scenario: *"We would drive to the person's house but Perley refused to deliver the check himself. He had me do it while he sat in the car. He got a kick out of my relating to him what the startled people said when I gave it to them with the explanation of who it was from, that it was real, and that there were no strings attached."*

Though Perley enjoyed giving to strangers in need, family came first. Although "old wounds" led him to skip over his children, he had no reservations about gifting his grandchildren and great-grandchildren. Despite favoring the girls, he also made sure his grandsons were supplied, though not quite as richly, with bank accounts from trust funds he set up. Whenever a land sale went through, someone's bank account grew. One such sale yielded $10,000 which Perley distributed among his youngest daughter's ten children. *"I have intended to give my more needy relatives, meaning mostly grandchildren, something to assist them,"* Perley said at the time. Perley ultimately gave thousands of dollars away to family, friends and strangers, keeping nothing more than a pittance to live on for himself. Habits run deep and he was, after all, a proper hermit.

Perley was especially satisfied when he could conduct legal business without relying on attorneys (and their fees) to finalize a transaction. At one point he shared uneven boundary lines with one of his neighbors, Dr. and Mrs. James Faulkner. To resolve the matter they decided to swap portions of their properties. *"The fact that they did this on a handshake and without the involvement of lawyers was particularly satisfying to Perley,"* recalled Anne Faulkner about her grandparent's transaction. *"In gratitude he sent a handwritten letter, a poem of sorts, to my parents, accompanied by passbooks for three savings accounts for my two sisters and me. I've heard he was similarly generous to others."*

During the summer of 1969, Perley was to meet and befriend the Weekes family from Long Island, New York. Seeking a weekend getaway from Madison Avenue, a place where they could spend "quality time" with their five children in a back-to-nature environment, Bob and Carol Weekes had rented Shinbone Shack on a year-round basis (an arrangement that would endure for another fifteen years). Many weekends and sometimes weeks at a time during summers were subsequently spent at "Shinbone" while their two sons and triplet daughters grew into and through their teenage years.

"Shinbone was a most curious place when we first discovered it," Bob recalled. "It had been unoccupied for many years and was in an advanced state of disrepair. It had no electricity, no water or plumbing and, blessedly, no telephone that could summon me back to my office in New York City. It was a place where a family – in order to survive – had to pull together, work together and, importantly, *be* together. We instantly loved it! We also became fascinated with the history of Shinbone, the nearby Lodge and with tales of Florence Brooks-Aten. And we soon learned that although we were recreating in a wilderness, we were not alone. A hermit named Perley Swett actually lived even *deeper* in these woods another mile up a rutted trail! So left to entertain ourselves in the middle of this wonderful nowhere, we resolved to meet this kindred spirit.

"Hiking up the washed out trail we spotted an old cape house atop a hill. It was surrounded by an overgrown and unfenced pasture where goats roamed at will. Coming closer we could see an old gentleman standing in the doorway, leaning on a walking stick and watching our approach as if he'd been expecting us. Not knowing whether our intrusion would be regarded kindly, I called out, "are you Perley Swett?"

"Might be," he answered cautiously. But there was something in his manner, a twinkle in his eye that made us think he'd welcome us if he found us worthy. Thus began a warm friendship that would last until Perley's death.

"We were fond of Perley from the start. Our triplet daughters were instantly comfortable with this old man whom they found to be warm, grandfatherly and genuinely interested in them. It wasn't until we had paid him a dozen or so visits that Perley confided to us that he had a special place in his heart for multiple births, having had twins himself. And we learned that our girls' birthday, July 15th, was Perley's wedding anniversary."

Perley was happy to have neighbors once again at Wood's Mill, especially neighbors who would visit during the lonely winter months. He was especially enthralled by the only (human) triplets, girls no less, he had ever encountered. He always enjoyed hearing their stories of life on Long Island and their experiences at Shinbone Shack. Betsy, Jenny and Julie would take turns sitting in his lap listening to his own tales of his life as a hermit. And they were openly affectionate toward him, occasionally throwing their arms around him and giving him kisses...the first he had received in more than thirty years.

And the gifts started coming. First they were hard candies wrapped in cellophane; then quarters and dollar bills. "Carol and I felt terrible," Bob explained. "How could our girls accept money from this impoverished old hermit who subsisted on goat's milk and Saltine Crackers?" But Perley would not be deterred.

"Don't the girls deserve it?," he'd ask. And that would be that!

To repay these kindnesses and being genuinely concerned about his health, the Weekes family regularly brought Perley groceries. "We'd tell him that they were left over from weekends at Shinbone and that he'd be doing us a real favor if he'd take them off our hands as we headed back to New York. That was the only way we could prevent him from trying to pay us for them."

"In the summer of 1972, just prior to the triplet's sixth birthday, *we received a call from Quentin White,*" Bob reminisced. *"He said Perley had some business to discuss with us. This struck us as odd but we assured Quentin we'd pay a visit soon. When we did, Perley handed the girls an envelope. Inside, written in his own hand and in stilted 'legalese' was a deed giving the girls a twenty-five acre parcel of land."*

Perley had bought this land in 1930, partly for sentimental reasons and partly as an investment. Coincidentally, it was along a section of the river which bordered this twenty-five acre lot where Perley's grandfather, Jonathan Whittier, had succumbed to exposure and died over one hundred years before. It also happened to be where Florence Aten had accidentally placed the northern end of the road she built so many years earlier to Shinbone Shack, land she unknowingly did not own at the time. *"Perley figured this out, knowing the land far better than Florence did, and bought it from the bank."* Bob explained, *"He wrote in the deed he gave the girls, 'this area seems very likely to become more valuable, and would seem might bring these girls a fairly good reserve to have in case of need later in life."*

Bob and Carol Weekes were, of course, dumbfounded that Perley would give their girls such a tremendous gift, but Perley assured them there was no point in arguing about accepting; the deed was already properly notarized and registered. *"Between girls being triplets (the only ones I ever expect to see) and the first girls to kiss me in over thirty years they hold a fairly warm place in my heart."*

Perley with Quentin White and his family
Notice the outhouse in background

Perley Swett

Perley and the Weekes triplets
Betsy, Julie and Jenny

Carol Weekes (mother of the triplets)
Being interviewed by Perley for "Housekeeper Wanted"

Chapter Twenty-One
Goodbye Dear Friend

Perley's life, at this late stage, had taken a definite turn. For almost forty years Perley had placed a distance between himself and the outside world, his way of dealing with possible rejection by others. Now, he was opening himself up to their companionship. Many of these new friends seemed genuinely interested in him, not simply because he was a curiosity - "The Hermit of Taylor Pond" - or even "Pearl Whittier, the poet," but because he was, simply, Perley Swett. They found him to be a kind and considerate human being. Once Perley learned to accept others, faults and all, he found they were more than willing to do the same for him.

It was becoming increasingly obvious to everyone but Perley that he should not be living alone. Several friends and relatives offered him a place in their homes but Perley did not want to leave his farm. At eighty-five he had become frail but Perley was determined that he would die on his own property as his mother, father, two grandfathers and baby brother had done.

Family and friends made it a point to call on Perley regularly. Quentin White's wife, Riita, called him every day to check on him. If she was unable to reach him after several tries, she would contact someone who might drive up to see if all was okay. Many times Quentin made the trek in to

Perley's isolated farm, sometimes on snowshoes late at night, to be sure Perley was all right.

On June 19, 1973, Riita tried all day to reach Perley by phone. Unable to contact anyone to go in and check on him, she waited until Quentin returned home the following day from a business trip. Though it was late in the evening, Quentin immediately set out to hike the three miles to Perley's farm, taking his young son with him.

As he approached the darkened house, Quentin felt increasingly uneasy. He called out to his old friend but there was no answer. They entered the house and stepped into the room where Perley slept, now forebodingly cold. Quentin described what he found over thirty years before as if it were yesterday: *"We found Perley on his little cot. He was badly dehydrated and dirty as the result of a stroke. He could not speak but was otherwise aware of everything. We gave him water, cleaned him and made him as comfortable as possible. He knew that he had had a stroke. He also knew that death would come. The two of us had talked about his upcoming death on several occasions. Perley had made it plain that when the time came he wanted nothing done to prolong his life. I had agreed if I were involved. I was in a dilemma. I knew of our agreement and I may have tried to honor it were it not for the presence of my young son. I told Perley that I should get him to a doctor and he let me know, even though he was unable to speak, that he did not want any part of that. I struggled with the problem and finally decided that I must move him out. I called the hospital for an ambulance and they referred me to the Keene Fire Department. They came up in a Power Wagon and took Perley out, with him objecting the whole way."* What Quentin did not realize at the time was that Perley, unable to talk, was frantically trying to tell him something.

Perley

Perley's greatest fear over the last few decades had been that he might die without making provisions for what would be done with his beloved home and 369 acre farm. Perley had always hoped that a family member would continue the one hundred year Swett family tradition and want to live there. However, it appeared very unlikely that any family member would be interested in living so deep in the woods in a house that would need to be totally rebuilt to be deemed livable.

A few years prior, on June 3, 1969, after much deliberation, Perley had made out a deed leaving the farm to four of his favorite people. These included two granddaughters and two good friends. Though he had the deed drawn up and "properly executed" by a lawyer, he never actually "delivered" it. And the New Hampshire Supreme Court states that a deed must be "delivered" to prove intent: *"If grantor does not want grantee to receive deed before death, he must give deed to someone else, or risk inference that deed was not delivered at all."* Very likely, Perley held off doing this to allow himself the freedom to change his mind. Perley always liked to keep his options open.

When the stroke left him partially paralyzed and unable to talk, and realizing that he was to be taken out of his home and brought to the hospital by Quentin, Perley became very insistent, almost frantic, motioning to the piles of papers heaped on his table. Both he and Quentin were frustrated by their inability to communicate. Not comprehending what Perley wanted on his table, Quentin was more concerned about keeping Perley calm and comfortable until the medics and four-wheel drive arrived. Quentin then rode to Keene with Perley, holding his hand the whole way.

Family and friends visited Perley in the hospital over the next few weeks. Perley's youngest daughter, Bernice and her family, along with the Whites, combined to keep a daily vigil by his bedside. The Weekes family headed North when they got the call that Perley was in the hospital. *"Tucked into a hospital bed miles from his homestead and unable to talk, his soulful eyes spoke volumes,"* Bob Weekes recalled. *"He squeezed each of our hands in turn and looked pleadingly at us. The man who had lived a life of total self-reliance was now utterly dependent on strangers for his survival. When we said our goodbyes that weekend before returning to New York we knew the end was near. Our girls gave him his usual goodbye kisses...only this time tears ran down his cheeks and ours."* Jenny Weekes, one of the triplets, remembered that experience years later: *"That was the only time I ever felt scared in his presence and that is because I knew how sick he was."*

Perley had told Quentin a few years earlier, that if anything ever happened to him, Quentin was to remove Perley's papers for safe keeping. When it became obvious that Perley would not be returning to his home, Quentin gathered and boxed up all of Perley's papers to preserve them from vandals who might be curious about treasures the hermit had left behind. Quentin made a quick look through Perley's papers to see if there was anything of importance, but with decades of documents to sift through, it would take months to search through everything and Quentin was already spending most of his free time at the hospital.

After a month of hospital care the doctors came to the conclusion that they could do no more for him and Perley was moved to a nursing home. He had not recovered the use of his right side or his speech. His worst fears had come to pass. Many years before, Perley had written in a letter to a friend saying: *"I would prefer a sudden death, rather than be helpless and a lingering death in a hospital."*

While Quentin kept a vigil by Perley's bedside it was apparent that Perley was still trying to communicate with Quentin about a matter of great urgency. Because Perley could not talk or write, Quentin had to guess at questions to ask him, trying to decipher his intent by searching for yes or no bodily responses. Not realizing there was a deed in Perley's papers and unaware of instructions that his missing will held, it was impossible for Quentin to make sense of what Perley was trying to tell him.

Perley stubbornly held on to life for over two months after his stroke. Confined to his bed, he finally succumbed to pneumonia. Without ever seeing his home again, Perley passed away quietly on September 1st, 1973.

Word spread quickly that "The Hermit of Taylor Pond" was no longer standing guard over his homestead. The few goats that were left were moved to a farm belonging to one of Perley's grandchildren.

Perley had previously made and paid for funeral arrangements which he insisted be kept as simple as possible. Despite that, some relatives already were objecting to Perley being buried in the grave he dug. They felt it was not proper and he should be buried in the family plot in the Sullivan, NH, cemetery next to his wife, precisely what Perley feared might happen. Fortunately, most of Perley's children, along with Quentin and other special friends, agreed that Perley should be buried on his farm in the grave he had dug. They threatened to make trouble if his wishes were not carried out.

The funeral was a simple service held at the United Church of Latter Day Saints in Keene. After the ceremony, Perley's plain casket was loaded not into a hearse but another four-wheel drive Dodge power wagon which led the funeral procession over the hills to return Perley to the place he was born.

Family and friends said their final goodbyes as Perley was lowered into his hand-dug grave. Finally, Perley had joined his baby brother and together they will keep eternal watch over his much-loved family farm.

Perley's image super-imposed over his house
Courtesy of John Bridges

One might think that Perley's story would end with his burial. At last he could rest contentedly, knowing his wish to remain on his farm had been granted. His family, however, was now faced with a major dilemma as a result of Perley being his own legal counsel. For he had left a Last Will and Testament, written partly in his own hand that would create a great deal of turmoil and cause the name "Perley Swett" to be remembered in legal channels for years to come.

There were already disagreements brewing in the family as to what was intended by Perley's confusing will. With many individual bequests and instructions listed, most of which were designed to favor some relatives and punish others, Perley had very carefully planned out the distribution of certain of his assets. However, in contrast to these meticulous instructions for relatively minor matters, not once did Perley mention how his homestead was to be disposed of other than to say, *"Unless changed, by me, disposition seems made of what is called the "home farm," and that seems to be around 369 acres."* What did Perley mean by this? As far as anyone knew he had not made any other provision for this property and yet he seemed to believe it had been properly taken care of. Certainly Perley was too careful a person to leave such an important issue unresolved.

This uncertainty kept the will tied up in probate court for the next year. In the meantime, Quentin finally conducted his search through Perley's papers and on November 21, 1974, over a year after Perley died, discovered the deed Perley had executed in 1969. Quentin immediately brought his discovery to the court's attention and more legal wrangling ensued.

Naturally, the four people named in the deed wanted it to be declared legal and binding. Other family heirs wanted it to be thrown out. After much debate, the case went to the Probate Court. Unable to settle the questions raised by the will, the will and deed were sent on to Superior Court.

If the deed was considered good, then Perley's remaining main asset, his home farm valued in 1974 at $100,000, would belong to the four people named. If the deed was deemed worthless, then the farm and land would pass back into the estate to be divided equally among the heirs. The question to be decided in Superior Court was whether Perley had ever actually "delivered" the deed to anyone to prove it was his final intent.

It was now up to the Superior Court to decide if Perley's act of motioning to the stack of papers on his table where the deed lay concealed constituted "delivery" to Quentin under the circumstances. Naturally, Perley's heirs argued that because he had, for years, left such an important document lying in a pile of other seemingly unimportant papers, it was likely that Perley had changed his mind and this was not his final decision of what he wanted done with his home.

The Superior court agreed with the heirs. It declared that the deed had never been delivered and therefore was null and void. This decision meant Perley's children would share in the distribution of his land. This was certainly not what Perley wanted as he repeatedly made it clear that he had no desire to see his children inherit any more of his land than what he had been forced to give to them almost forty years before.

His intention shows clearly in a letter he wrote, but again may not have sent, in 1971: *"to whom it may concern - In case my heirs feel ill-used because of my disposing of considerable of my property and giving some to friends, instead of giving it, or leaving it for my heirs to quarrel over, for several reasons I feel justified in so doing."* As one local lawyer summed it up in retrospect: *"Perley's actions stand as the example of how NOT to handle your affairs if you want your wishes followed after death."*

But the issue was still not settled. Unwilling to accept the verdict of the Superior Court, the recipients named in the deed brought the case to the New Hampshire Supreme Court. Twenty pages of detailed information were sent to the Supreme Court for the answer to one question: *"Did title to the premises described therein pass to the grantees of the executed unrecorded deed dated June 3, 1969, found among decedent's papers?"*

It was now up to the Supreme Court to make the final decision. Perley had been dead and buried for four years and the disposition of his estate was still unresolved. After deliberation, it was the final decision of the Supreme Court that Perley did indeed make delivery of the deed as he lay on his cot after suffering his stroke. In the only way possible for him at the time, the court reasoned that Perley "delivered" the deed to Quentin when he motioned to the pile of papers on his table.

This Supreme Court decision became a landmark case. Perley, once again, added to his own legend since the principles of this court case would be taught in law schools across the country for years to come. And to bring closure to his long and lonely journey, Perley could finally claim that he won - if posthumously - his first legal battle.

Perley Edwin Swett
Courtesy of John Bridges

A Final Visit

On a golden spring morning in the year 2000, almost thirty years after his death, I, and several members of my family, including my eighty-four year old father, Perley's son, Maurice, all loaded into our vehicles to caravan our way to Grampa's old homestead. The last time I had been there was for his funeral in 1973.

We traveled several miles and many years back. The narrow dirt road seemed only a little better cared for than the one I remembered. Though the encroaching forest bordering the road had grown much thicker, the few houses that dotted the wayside were in better shape than they had been years before. Considering the amount of expansion and development taking place in other parts of town, this neighborhood had changed very little over the years and our journey was remarkably similar to what I remembered as a child.

On our way to Grampa's we stopped first at "Schoolhouse #3" located at what was once Seward Farm, almost three miles from Grampa's house. We toured the primitive one-room school built in 1849. My father sat at the same wooden desk where he had carved his initials almost eighty years before and shared some anecdotes.

"*This was the school where my father and his siblings once attended, walking the 2 ½ miles from their home. The town of Stoddard allowed my grandparents $5.00 a year to be spent on shoe leather.*" With a faraway glint in his eyes he continued, *"With no heat other than a woodstove, someone would have to get to the school an hour earlier than the teacher and other students to get the fire going and warm things up. Usually that was left to one of the oldest boys. I did it the last year I was here."*

My father spoke in his low and steady voice. The rest of us stopped talking to listen so we wouldn't miss anything he had to say. At eighty-four we knew without anyone voicing the thought that any stories Dad shared could be his last. He continued: *"Every Memorial day we used to learn poems or plays to recite at the church, where all the town schools met to celebrate. After services we would all march down to the cemetery and girls would distribute flags to all the veterans' graves."* I was glad my own sons, Jake and Sam, had a chance to hear their grandfather reminisce about those times.

We continued on our way and my father pointed out to the youngest members of the family where "the old Hasting's farm" had been. For that was the site of the house he grew up in. Now another house stood there, my father's home having long since fallen in and been removed.

A short distance further we came to the junction in the road where a now overgrown and abandoned trail led to Shinbone Shack and the estate where Florence Brooks-Aten had invested so much of her money and her time to build a home in a wilderness setting at the old Wood's Mill. In 1990 the "Lodge" and 225 acres were sold to Don and Joyce Healy, a couple from New York who, through a separate set of circumstances, had also fallen in love with the land. They began extensive renovations and by the year 2001 had put the finishing touches on, as Perley once described it, Florence's "Unfinished Dream."

* * *

The reader might appreciate a slight digression from the story at this point. It concerns a remarkable set of circumstances that occurred as I was wrapping up the final details on this book. The question remains, what happened to the long lost portrait of Florence Brooks-Aten painted by noted artist George de Forest Brush in 1925? This painting had disappeared seventy-seven years earlier when the New York State Supreme Court ruled in 1930 against Mrs. Aten in the civil suit brought by the artist seeking payment. Perhaps it was sold with Florence's other possessions to raise money for her creditors. And now, incredibly, the painting was about to be rediscovered in the spring of 2007 through a most unlikely set of coincidences.

Charles Cobb, a respected auctioneer in Peterborough, New Hampshire, was about to hold another of his catalogued sales of antiques and art. Bob Weekes, whose family had rented Shinbone Shack for fifteen years (and who has assisted me as editor of this book), is a life-long collector of art and antiques. Having done business with Mr. Cobb in the past, he received a complimentary copy of the catalog in the mail. Thumbing through it, Bob was stunned to find himself staring at a thumbnail photo of Item #113. It was a portrait of a woman bearing a striking resemblance to Florence Brooks-Aten! Due to his work editing my manuscript Bob was familiar with the story of Florence's missing portrait. His eyes flew to the description: "a seated woman wearing pearls, unknown sitter." And the artist whose signature appeared in the painting? George de Forest Brush! The description ended with the clincher, a notation that on the back of the portrait were two labels identifying the painting as evidence in a 1930 New York State Supreme Court case.

Given the unlikelihood that the painting would be discovered and recognized by one of the few people on the planet who knew something of its history and had also seen the few faded photographs of Florence Aten that existed, one has to believe in serendipity. And the story has a serendipitous ending. Bob immediately contacted Don Healy, the owner of Florence's estate, who purchased the painting at auction and, eighty-two years after it had been painted, returned it to its intended place of honor at her beloved lodge.

* * *

As we passed the trail to Shinbone Shack and drove up the incline to Grampa's house, I almost (but not quite) missed having his herd of goats circling our vehicle. Our family no longer owned Grampa Perley's 369-acre farm. But he would have been pleased that the current owners also have a deep love of the land and have tried to maintain the area much as it was when he owned it. They have done a beautiful job of preserving the original design of the house through a total renovation.

Upon arriving at our destination and after exchanging pleasantries, Anne Faulkner, the new owner, graciously gave us a tour of her home. She described in loving detail the remodeling she and her husband had done over the previous few years. She had met Grampa when she was a young child and, like most people who knew him, had warm memories: *"I was a very young child, probably 5 or 6, when I met Perley. He was a kind and welcoming old man. He brought out the Saltines for us to feed the goats. I think he shared candy with us and let us play on his treadmill."*

Though I knew the house had been totally rebuilt from the framework out after Grampa died, it was done in a way that rekindled vivid memories. I could swear I remembered a particular cabinet or doorway, architectural features that once were almost obscured by my grandfather's "collections." It was exciting now to see what the house might have looked like in earlier days, though I had a feeling that although authentically reproduced, Perley's house had never looked quite this good.

After concluding our tour, we shared memories around the large central dining room table, now strangely bare of clutter, with a pitcher of lemonade and some of Anne's home-baked oatmeal cookies. *"I think this is the first time I have ever seen sunlight streaming through this room,"* my brother Frank commented. Nodding our heads in agreement, we explained to the younger members of our family how dark and gloomy the house had always been when we visited Grampa. At that time, the two small windows in the kitchen were so thick with dirt and soot from the woodstove and years of accumulated grime that very little light ever penetrated, even on a bright sunny day. Today the glorious spring sunshine was bursting through several larger, newly installed and <u>clean</u> windows. Once again, the Whittier/Swett Homestead was full of life.

After sharing our memories of Grampa we walked through the fields, where my brothers and father once spent many hours cutting the hay. We followed the worn path down through the woods, now much thicker than I remembered, to Taylor Pond where my family had enjoyed many relaxing afternoons fishing for the string of 'junk' fish we pulled out. Once again we stood on the big rock by the shore overlooking the water. It seemed so familiar and yet the rock we stood on didn't seem quite as large as the one I remembered as a child. The pond also seemed a little smaller and more overgrown with weeds and lily pads. I could hardly believe almost forty years had passed since I had stood at this same spot wearing my brother's over-sized plaid flannel shirt and holding one of our old fishing poles. I remember squealing with delight when I swung a "pumpkinseed" over my brother's head to land in my father's hands so he could take it off the hook.

A Final Visit

Finally we walked back up the path to Grampa's unmarked grave. As he had instructed, there was nothing commemorating the site. *"If marked as a grave perhaps fifty years in the future,"* Grampa had instructed, *"some party might have a summer home here and not desire a grave close to their house or lawn. Better in such a case for them not to know of it."*

Only the large granite boulder still nestled between several much bigger birch trees gave any indication that this was the spot that Grampa chose as his final resting place. For a few minutes we stood in quiet contemplation. Struck by the serenity and beauty of this chosen gravesite, I knew without a doubt this was the right place for Grampa to spend eternity.

This was a very memorable and poignant return for me to Grampa's farm. My own father, Maurice Swett, died later that same year in December, 2000. He was eighty-five, the same age as Perley when he passed on. Suddenly I realized that there were very few people left to ask about the past. I had lost my most valuable resource of information with my father's death. If I wanted to understand Grampa's story I could not wait any longer, it was time to begin my journey...

* * *

After almost seven years of researching and writing this book and exploring the history of my ancestors, I have acquired a much deeper respect for, and understanding of, the trials they faced and the times in which they lived. And I believe I have come to know much better the mindset and reasoning of a true nineteenth century throwback, The Hermit of Taylor Pond. Though Grampa would live most of his life in the twentieth century, he would cling doggedly to the values and lifestyle of an earlier time. A product of his upbringing, he would struggle through life with honor

Perley

because, to him, there was no other way. And while I and my readers may not condone some of the actions he took, I understand much better now why he felt compelled to follow the path he chose.

Even now, thirty-five years after his death, I am often asked if I am related to Perley Swett, the Hermit of Taylor Pond. And I always answer with pride, "Yes, he was my Grandfather."

Sam Thompson (son of the author) checking the desk where his grandfather, Maurice, and possibly great-grandfather, Perley, once sat

Anne Faulkner, Frank Swett, Jr. standing, and Maurice Swett reminiscing at kitchen table

Perley's house during renovations - 1979
Original restoration work done by Geoff Howard

After remodeling in 1986

Keene Sentinel newspaper picture of Florence Brooks Aten
And her "missing" portrait painted by George de Forest Brush

Florence's renovated lodge in 2002
Courtesy of Don and Joyce Healy

Some postscripts from people who knew Perley

Quentin White: "After a nearly full lifetime of interesting events and experiences, I remember Perley E. Swett as an extraordinary friend who gave meaning to me and my family during our stay in New England. He taught us much and blessed our lives. I am happy that Sheila (Swett) Thompson has put this record into print. Others may now come to know this commonly good man."

Ernest Hebert, Keene native and award winning author: "I think what appealed to me about Perley was his individualism. I'd never met anyone like him before. I liked the complexity of his personality; a hermit who appeared to need people. I liked his sense of humor. Perley was, in part, the inspiration for the character Cooty Patterson in my books."

Alan F. Rumrill, Director of the Historical Society of Cheshire County: "My family and Perley's family were acquainted from the early days of Stoddard. When I was a boy my mother would occasionally lead my sister and I on hikes from Granite Lake through the woods to visit Perley. During one such trek we entered his house through the dark shed and into Perley's kitchen/office/living space to visit. Just inside the room, at my eye level, was a table piled high with a wide assortment of paraphernalia. On what seemed to be the only uncluttered surface was a dead mouse laid out perfectly straight. My young mind imagined it as Perley's supper!

Perley's eyes were often bright and cheerful, but on occasion they seemed to be tinged with melancholy. As a young boy, and in the many times that I have thought of Perley since then, I never understood how his own experiences led him to a solitary life in the woods of Stoddard. Sheila's story illuminates the journey of this alternately cheerful and melancholy man who was proudly claimed by his hometown as "the hermit of Taylor Pond."

Daniel Swett, grandson and author of *Hypothetical Mishmash*, a book of poetry: "I was young then and perhaps did not fully appreciate the complexity of the man or the simplicity of his life, but well do I remember in high school telling my classmates, with pride, of Perley's lifestyle which to me made him far more of a "real" hermit than those that we read about in class. It was perhaps thanks to Perley's lifelong dream to see his poetry published that inspired me to write a book of poetry."

Pat McMahon Clark of Stoddard: "Why do some people appear larger than life, endlessly fascinate the local populace and become the stuff of legends and myths? Perley Swett assuredly attained that status in his life and remains a mythical presence many years after his death. Stories of eccentricities and misadventures permeated my growing up years in East Sullivan and come to mind even now whenever his name is mentioned."

Linda Fish Brown, special friend and longtime correspondent of Perley's: "An old house in Stoddard in need of repair; a Sears catalog; a lifelong friendship - and a unanimous State of New Hampshire Supreme Court decision. Perley E. Swett was - and remains to this day - an important, positive and significant part of a New Hampshire girl's life. Many memories, many stories, many poems - my friend."

From the Weekes Family...

Julie (triplet): "When I think of Perley I'm reminded of a warm July day when he shared our birthday cake, sitting on a stone wall across the lane from his house. He encouraged my sisters and I to appreciate not just the view, but life itself. I still marvel at how a man with so little had so much to offer."

Betsy (triplet): "Perley exemplified optimism. Despite his sometimes dour view of the world, his very existence offered proof that we have within us the ability to remain strong and independent and to enjoy life regardless of what it hands us."

Jenny (triplet): "Looking back as an adult, I realize that there was much about Perley and his rundown homestead that could have made a young girl of six apprehensive. Yet as a child I never felt that way. I didn't understand why he lived alone as a hermit but I sensed that he'd been through some rough times and was simply doing the best that he could under very difficult circumstances. And that impressed me greatly."

Bob (father of the triplets): "All of us can look back on people we've known who touched us in special ways. For my wife and children, Perley Swett was one of them. Although he lived in the sparest of circumstances, we felt Perley needed only one thing to survive. And that was to have somebody love him. And we did."

Perley Edwin Swett - The Hermit of Taylor Pond
Taken October 1968
Courtesy of Ernie Hebert

Perley's Poetry

Perley

A Testimonial to "Campbell Soup Company"

This "Poet" were sorry to learn that one of your
    Farm work horses were recently lost;
But he hope that it will not mean that your
    Beef soups may be raised in cost.
Yet it might appear your loss may mean the
    Consumers have now seemingly gained;
For those small cans of "vegetable beef soup," a
    Little extra meat seem now to have contained.

Meat being more scarce in recent years, as well as
    The price being so extremely high;
Surely your employees cannot be blamed if to
    Earn their weekly wage they might try,
But when a farm horse breaks a leg, and so much
    Meat then seems liable to go to waste;
"Vegetable beef soup" can have a much better supply
    Of meat instead of perhaps hardly enough to taste.
Maybe this information were wrong, and all the
    Farm horses are perhaps being killed;
As they were not needed anymore, as farm tractors
    Their places have doubtless now filled.
So the horses are being disposed of as fast as in
    "beef" soups they can seem to be sold.
But this customer surely hope they will be cooked
    Enough to be tender, if any are tough or old.

For he is now "along in years" and all his teeth
    For quite a few years have been gone;
Therefore only tender meat or food that needs
    Less "chewing" seems what he now live on
And though blessed with over thirty descendants

Perley's Poetry

For over twenty years he has lived alone,
In the old house where he were born, and though
    Perhaps a "famous hermit," as a "poet" seems
    still unknown.

Somewhat over two cases yearly, of your soups
    During recent years has been bought,
"Vegetable beef" the favored brand especially
    Lately, as more meat seems now to be got.
But if the meat content may later be made less,
    So hardly more than a taste can be found;
One might just as well live mostly on vegetables
    Which one can raise on a small plot of any rich ground.

Many other companies make soups but the name
    Campbell sounds a little the best;
For it seems an old Scotch name once very famous,
    That later spread to England and the West,
Surely those that left their native lands and
    To the "Western world" many years ago came;
Though now engaged in a "canning industry," are
    Not detracting their ancestors glorious fame.

If you wish to use this letter as a "testimonial," no
    Specified money charge there can be;
But if "generous hearted" you might give this old
    "poet" an order to get a case of soup free.
Twice as much of your beef soup might be used if
    Money came in just a little more fast;
Alas more of your beans, if more pork were put
    In, than has been found in any can in the past.

Perley

"Pork and beans" on the can label reads good
    But the pork content seems too small;
When a pig, born in the spring, can easily make
    Two hundred pounds of pork, in the fall.
So please have more put in those cans, even if
    Perhaps your profit may be a little lowered;
But above all else, keep the prices sufficiently
    Low so the poorer people "Campbell's products"
        can afford.

Doubtless horsemeat is "just as good," and a small
    "soup of beef" is all a can need to contain;
To be labeled "vegetable beef soup," that seems to
    Be printed on each can label very plain,
Other Campbell products are also used, but these
    Two herein mentioned are favored the more;
And are usually bought by the case, and most
    Generally got at the East Sullivan "Village Store."

Very thankful this old "poet" will be, if instructions to
    Your employees you might very soon give;
To at least double the pork in your "pork and beans;"
    And aid the poorer people to better live.
No matter if horsemeat, or beef cattle also raise
    The meat content, as much as can well be done;
In those cans of "vegetable beef soup" and the main
    Purpose of this letter will then seem to have been won.

Yet if you feel inclined to go by the old time
    Maxim, that it is better to give than to receive;
Some of your products would be welcome, if you
    Cared to aid the government, "poverty to relieve,"
But another reason for this letter is because it
    Helps pass away quite a few hours of time;

For a man, not exactly crippled, but now too
    Old, or lazy, for real work, but laziness
        (at any age) seems to be no crime.

Your products have always seemed good, but he
    Hopes these favored ones be even better made;
Without raising the cost, for many people go
    By the price tag more than by the grade,
And not being over-burdened with wealth this
    "Poet" admits he goes by the price tag as well;
So it seems the cheaper one can produce good
    Stuff (of any kind) the more one can expect to sell.

Pearl Whittier
(Perley Swett)
4-3-67

Perley

Stoddard History in Verse
By Pearl Whittier (Perley Swett)
Written around 1935

My grandad moved to Stoddard nearly fourscore years ago;
He came not in an auto truck, but with a yoke of oxen slow.
He worked and slaved and worried and tried hard to succeed,
And died not quite a pauper, but with a family left in need.
Twas the first hard storm that winter; a blizzard, nothing more;
He went to the nearest village that boasted a country store,
They had to have provisions, all alone and afoot he went,
He got them and started homeward, they cost his last red cent.

His family was worried and hungry and waited for him all night.
And never knew until next May he died with his home in sight.
They searched many days that winter but the drifts were terrible deep,
They found him when the snow was gone and the frogs began to peep.
His wife hung onto the homestead, two daughters live there still;
But the grandchildren left the rocky place against their parent's will,
They are living in New England, except one in a distant state.
Some have children, all are married, but one who lost her mate.

Farming is the lowest lot God in his grace ever gave,
My grandfather found that out before he went to his grave.
I own the land on which he died and on which he strove to live,
To be something beside a farmer most anything I would give.
A banker or a merchant or a garage man would be fine,
Or even to be a poet like that distant cousin of mine,
If he had written these verses they would not be so bad,
If I had a sunny disposition I should not feel so sad.

Perley

"Snow Bound"
Or
Stoddard History in Verse

The title of Whittier's poem I have here taken,
    But being related he doubtless would not care;
For a snow covered scene kindred hearts awaken,
    Even though a difference of opinion they share.

The fences like in John's story, are well covered,
    And the white drifts piled high all around;
Should death come how long before it were discovered,
    Deeply snowed in and completely "snow bound."

Were my cousin alone and blocked in so tightly,
    In that poem more of worry may have shown;
Though admitting the clean snow is very sightly,
    Often too much with a shovel must be thrown.

With a barn and house on speaking terms only,
    And up to four feet all the way snow between;
In that section of a township now wild and lonely,
    Two miles from a neighbor and no house to be seen.

Once by neighbors these old timers were surrounded,
    Within my memory the last half have slowly gone;
Sheep, cows and oxen in large number abounded,
    But the farms were deserted as the old folks passed on.

Perhaps the Sewards and Hastings more land longer held,
    Yet mostly where Stoddard had given another town;
Whittiers came only after Greenes and Taylors sold,
    Even their names are gone except where written down.

Perley's Poetry

Perhaps no one about this desertion is complaining,
    If now other jobs and better locations are preferred;
Yet wild life with the woods and brush is gaining,
    With both bear and panther at times seen or heard.

The last resident in this district were my mother,
    My father was older and twenty years had been dead;
Now I try to farm this place rather than another,
    Where a spring breeze leveled my barn and shed.

That was the Hastings' homestead, in long ago years,
    But had passed through other hands were by me run;
Yet the house with its big five flue chimney rears,
    Still a monument to what these old settlers had done.

A four foot shingle forty rods away was standing,
    Driven into the ground with considerable force;
While the barn roof made three layers when landing,
    Just a young and very playful wind, of course.

These old timers used real lumber in their building,
    Mortised braces with all the timbers rough hewn;
Outside surfaces could seldom boast of gilding,
    Leveled completely and over acres much was strewn.

A good path to travel is always badly needed,
    Between water at house and barn where it never flow;
Doubtless such matters were forgot or unheeded,
    In those verses telling of the drifted white snow.

But I heard that poem helped John G. get started,
    Less perhaps to wealth than the road to fame;
Maybe too much snow has made me downhearted,
    And as I feel must need to write the same.

Perley

No claim do I make as a poet, or expect ever to see,
    My name added to a list who are as poets classed;
So what I write may be forgot, as I expect to be,
    Before all those now living from this life have passed.

Perhaps damage by storms that have come in my time,
    Has caused too much prejudice to very easily fade;
Yet to take a different view can hardly be a crime,
    And should not any part of their beauty degrade.

The hurricane fell a shed and top off the chimney shook,
    On my mother's place where I now make my home;
Yet through the woods a sweet vengeance it took,
    Where frisky and happy it very playfully roam.

Blocked now by two storms and unplowed still,
    Over two miles to the nearest opened highway;
Passable only on snowshoes or perhaps skis until,
    This road might be plowed but when hard to say.

And though our fine scenery is often highly praised,
    It is in the summer when seen by the most;
Still I have a fondness for where I was raised,
    But of winter scenes let the real poets boast.

While I stick to the farm and may not interfere,
    Unless to express opinion the urge gets too strong;
The snow may be beautiful, but much that comes here,
    Comes too deep or too fierce and lasts far too long.

Only once in five weeks now to the village store,
    Have I been to get groceries, any bread or mail;
With the post office over five miles from my door,
    And often in winter foot travel must prevail.

By a Stoddard blizzard a grandparent were blinded,
    On his homeward way and his life had to give;
When younger the same walks were less minded,
    And on this Hastings farm nearer to town I did live.

Some of the windows the snow partially darken,
    Driven by the wind against the house to embank;
And to my prayers God seems never to hearken,
    Whether I curse the snow or for a favor try to thank.

But too much of some things steadily to face,
    No matter when or where may get a person's goat;
And this is a much different time and place,
    From that in which the original poem was wrote.

Yet with a house to shelter and food of some kind,
    No backwoods farmer has any rights to complain;
For if the world were looked over, its miseries to find,
    Better would be appreciated both the snow and rain.

Perhaps being too much alone a difference make,
    For often in winter as a hermit I could be styled;
But what is sent by God one should cheerfully take,
    Even a New Hampshire storm both rough and wild.

        By Pearl Whittier
        (with apologies to John G. for
        Using title of his poem)
        Dated 3/5-6-7/1947

Perley

The Unfinished Dream

"Wood's Mill and Chandler Meadows, N.H.,"- has that not a pretty sound?
In old times to fishermen, it was known for miles around.
T'was a good place in the ancient times,- a place to keep in mind;
And t'was there that old Staunch Water Mill sawed timber of all kind.
All the houses in that section were made from timbers from this mill;
Of which little remains but the old water wheel is still.

Wood's Mill has not been run for thirty-five years and maybe more,
But even then it was falling down with a very unsafe floor.
Houses stood up better then; years it's been since the last fell in.
And all the barns had gone before as they were never built too strong.
One way in is "discontinued,"- Stoddard fixes that road no more;
And over the hill, the old stage-coach road to Munsonville was given up long before.

Chandler built the upper dam long before the woods were born;
And the brook flowed the meadow for a mile, where earlier they raised corn.
Everything now, there is to see, is where the dam once stood.
No one remembers Chandler, where he built, what it was, or how good.
I think that he once ran a grist mill built at the upper dam,

And ground out grain in sun and rain; four mill stones left the trace.

Wood was a later man,- who came after others had built,
And it seems a funny thing; the place goes by his name.
The man who built this historic spot is unknown to folks around.
Perhaps in the town history it could be found.

Since Wood's Mill was so long deserted and no one living there,
T'was called the "Haunted Village,"
Used by rowdies and no one seemed to care
How drunk they got or even what they did.
It was, I think, a dirty shame, to use for such
A place with this pretty name.
Wood's Mill of historic fame shall never be abused by rowdies as of yore,
And now signs may be found: "Keep off" and "Come no more."

A new dam holds the waters above,- that which ran the mill,
New buildings dot the landscape, with the old trees around them still.
A new leading to the lake from the Concord Road;
Stone bridges cross the brooks,- that hold a ten ton load.
A new building called a Power Plant that's also built of stone.
This new house will stay till a future day, when it will stand alone.

Wood's Mill of the future, for you what has God in store?
And Wood's Mill Manor you are called, t'was Shinbone Shack before.

Perley

A mansion large and stately,- a garden with stone walls in the sun,
Was built beside your waters, but never quite got done.

By Pearl Whittier
Around 1932

A Parody of Two Poems

With his feet in the open oven slowly warming,
    And a sweater and heavy coat on his back;
Praying it may soon stop so fiercely storming,
    For nearly buried the small one story shack.

Strong winds drifting the white snow all around,
    The well trod path, to the barn hard to keep;
No telephone to use, broken wires on the ground,
    Road badly blocked and still getting more deep.

Far back in the woods and no electricity here,
    Too expensive a luxury to put in for one place;
Bad hills for good cars, anytime of the year,
    So when deer hunting season is over, solitude he face.

Considerable groceries on hand, also wood in the sheds,
    Fairly well prepared against starvation or to freeze;
In possession of the old Whittier brothers' homesteads,
    But now too feeble to travel on snow shoes or skies.

Over two miles, if he tried anyone to see or contact,
    For Taylor Pond region has long been termed wild;
Not in a poet's imagination but snowbound in fact,
    This old hermit, now living where raised as a child.

Wondering if it might be his last birthday,
    And Longfellow being dead for a long time;
No one any good words about him, to say,
    Like were said, of John Greenleaf, in rhyme.

Perley

But perhaps inherited the inclination verse to write,
    As a cousinship to the "Quaker Poet: can be claimed;
Evening composing helps also to shorten a winter night,
    Preferring also to be as poet, more than as a hermit, famed.

From his family much divorced and friends very few,
    Many believing Heaven his reach far beyond;
Not many caring if he still live, or ever really knew,
    This old Stoddard native, born near Taylor's fish pond.

Yet before in the ground his body may be covered,
    For his worldly goods, a battle royal might start;
Even his will try to break, as soon as it were discovered,
    Claiming his mind were much weaker than his heart.

Just a hermit usually called, that preferred to live alone,
    Unlearned all else about him that may have been said;
But that he sometimes wrote poetry were quite well known,
    For much too truthful some of the stories they read.

No songs of praise about him, any children ever sing,
    And slanderous gossip can seldom be called fame;
The winds howling around none of this seem to bring,
    While very little comfort in the mails ever came.

His poetry were invariably returned (if postage were sent),
    Just the few poems that to have published he try;
Doubtless John G. never really knew what being snowbound meant,
    And had many friends all around him when he died.

"Wrote several years ago. Copied from memory. By the old Taylor Pond Hermit. It seems a double apology is due both Henry W. Longfellow and John G. Whittier (for 'slandering' their very nice poems.)"

By Pearl Whittier
Dated 2-2-1967

Perley

Taylor Pond, the Brook and Small Farm by their Shore

Just a small and semi-private area of fishing ground today,
For the bog and swamp lands are no longer flowed;
Rocky or grassy shores, but deep mud more of the way,
And the pond is nearly half a mile from the road.

Taylor brook is by this crossed, over a double sluiceway of stone,
Only a small streamlet; but trout and turtle are here seen;
Further down it joins another, that as Otter River seems known,
Still growing larger as it flows onward toward Keene.

In Taylor pond good fish of several kinds are found,
And wild duck raise their young ducklings without fear;
For pout the muddy parts make good breeding ground,
While the wooded shores furnish abundant shelter for deer.

Nearby a wild and deep forest, when the Taylors first came,
To settle on this land bordering their eastern shore;
From this pioneer family these waters got their name,
Where the Taylors farmed one hundred years and more.

Near the first falls they built a dam and then a mill,
And fenced much field and pasture land with stone wall;
But though their old and rocky homestead is occupied still,
Like the pond's area, the tillage land has grown more small.

The mill was moved away, and the dam has gone out,
And for much hard labor only stone work now show;
But two buildings yet stand, and a few acres still about,
Furnish feed when the ground is covered with snow.

Whittiers bought this farm, the Taylor family had cleared,
And for a few years only were it ever rented or loaned;
So to the present owner it seems to be more endeared,
For since settled, by these two families it were owned.

This buyer only a few years did here reap and sow,
As he failed to return with one load of groceries he bring;
Just a rough December storm, and it seemed he had to go,
But was found only when snow had settled in the spring.

The present owner cannot hope this full century to live,
And may need to die on this farm and still alone;
For two miles in any direction a compass may give,
Scores of old farms are deserted, and mostly overgrown.

One schoolhouse location could now be found by very few,
Yet Taylor pond will remain, and other landmarks as well;
To it's high peak, in one century, southwest Stoddard grew,
But long before the second ends, to one resident has fell.

Southwest Stoddard formerly raised many cattle and sheep,
And field crops of many kinds, and even wheat grain;
But Stoddard winters are quite severe, and snow often deep,
Yet this quick rise, and swifter fall, is still hard to explain.

Many miles of roads closed, and no one can tell why,
Unless appeal of city attractions were too hard to withstand;
But in some cases an added burden for charity to supply,
Where unemployed have no cash, or any reserve on hand.

Few now are those willing to live in a back country home,
Bears and panther already have been heard here or seen;
Moose also, and even wolves over these farms may again roam,

Perley

Surely a good hunting ground, and not too far from Keene.

Perhaps two extra miles, these hunters may later need to walk,
For this road, and last resident, are in the same class;
The last occupied farm, and buildings, with a few head of stock,
Into the hands of non-residents, and strangers, may soon need to pass.

Perhaps this fate can be postponed, by offering this old farm title free,
To the right party who may consent to live here all their life;
Youth and courage they would need, and to give this guarantee,
And then one might secure this homestead by becoming a farmer's wife.

                    Pearl Whittier
                    Dated 2-27-1950